Praise for *The Magic of Metaphor*

"I have looked through the collection and have been both excited and uplifted by what I've found. I think that this is a very valuable resource for all teachers, trainers and facilitators. The stories themselves are rich and varied, and contain all the seeds of transformative learning – open-endedness, dramatic tension, humour and above all, the possibility of multiple interpretations. All of these qualities will enable teachers to develop dialogue and discussion with their learning groups on a wide range of issues. The narrative approach also facilitates the development of thinking skills, tapping into our resources of intuition and imagery. The narrative techniques are thus suitable for use both in language learning and development, as well as in training contexts. In addition to the valuable stories, I find the sections on their use and the rationale for their use both clear and accessible. Nick Owen has produced a book which deserves many users and a wide audience."
– **Dr. Tony Wright**, Principal Lecturer, International Education, College of St. Mark & John, Plymouth.

"I love the book, both in terms of its content and the style in which it is written. The Master and Apprentice dialogue reminds me of *The Little Prince*, a great book about learning, and this dialogue provides added meaning and relevance to the stories. The variety in the stories provides a huge source of material for anyone who seeks to influence or entertain others through story telling. Some made me laugh, others were so clever I had to show them to others, and the spiritual depth of many I found very thought provoking."
– **Richard Holroyd**, Head of Training & Development, Hong Kong Shanghai Banking Corporation.

"Stories have historically been an excellent way of getting messages across to a wide audience. This book gives the communicator a refreshing and creative way of cutting through the language barrier of Information Technology and delivering clear messages to often diverse audiences."
– **Alison Hood**, Managing Consultant and Operations Director for the Wholesale Investment Banking Practice.

"Nick Owen has managed to put together a collection of fascinating stories. His book does not only live up to Egan Kieran's dictum that the story 'is not just some casual entertainment; it reflects a basic and powerful form in which we make sense of the world and experience.' (*Teaching as Story Telling*, 1986) The stories in this book offer more than orientation. They serve as blueprints for future action and are an elegant means of transformation and change. *The Magic of Metaphor* is a brilliant book. I can highly recommend it."
– **Dr. Herbert Puchta**, author and NLP Master Practitioner.

"A treasure trove of wisdom and fun! Stories for leaders to use on every occasion to enhance their effectiveness."
– **Richard D Field OBE**, Industrialist, Leadership Coach and Student.

"Nick has collected some great stories here and put them together in a way which is really useful for speakers and trainers. I particularly like the material about how to improve our storytelling techniques. I shall certainly be using this book on our NLP trainings and leadership seminars, and recommending it to all trainers."
– **Peter McNab**, INLPTA Master Trainer, Director of EFA (Training & Consultancy) Ltd., Founder Member of the Integral Institute.

"The stories, parables and myths in *The Magic of Metaphor* lend support to understanding and have a central didactic value. Many people feel overwhelmed when confronted with the abstract aspects of psychotherapeutic topics. One way to make it easier to understand is to use an example, a mythological story … or an imagination. In their own way these all deal with personal, interpersonal and social conflicts, and present possible solutions. The stories in this book, if used in a conscious way, help to gain a more distanced relationship to conflicts. The item 'individual mythology and magic' is understood to refer to all concepts as crystallisation of the attitudes of the individual. The effective mythology and magic, on the other hand, compromises conflicts which are detached from the individual and have acquired a social reality in communication and tradition. This book will not only be relevant just to those with professional interactive psychotherapy, it is also a rich treasure of psychological and pedagogic insights for others."
– **Professor Nossrat Peseschkian**, Director of the Wiesbadener fur Psychotherapie, Germany.

"I think the book is a fine offering to the teaching and training world."
– **Judith DeLozier**, author, NLP developer.

"The book appeals on diverse levels with insights and enlightening illustrations that will illuminate teaching and learning. Drawn from ancient oriental traditions, contemporary sources and the author's own repertoire – the experience is challenging, life-affirming and enriching."
– **Mick Reid**, Voluntary Service Overseas, London.

"When Nick is training, his genuine love for and pride in his work really shines through. He is generous in his wish to share his knowledge and skills with others. He uses storytelling to great effect, capturing his audience with an abundance of multisensory language and the rich tones in his voice. A shared common experience enables all those who listen to become completely absorbed, connecting with their unconscious minds as they do so. Each person discovering often long after the story has finished that they keep pondering about what it meant for them. 'Get your rocks in first' is now a well established catch phrase embedded in the culture of our organisation … that's a powerful result after telling a story once to a group of staff."
– **Carolyn Temple BDS, MSc, DDPH, RCS**, Director of Community and Priority Services, Chester and Halton Community NHS Trust.

The Magic of
Metaphor
77 Stories for Teachers,
Trainers & Thinkers

Nick Owen

Crown House Publishing Limited
www.crownhouse.co.uk
www.crownhousepublishing.com

First published by
Crown House Publishing Ltd
Crown Buildings, Bancyfelin, Carmarthen, Wales, SA33 5ND, UK
www.crownhouse.co.uk

and

Crown House Publishing Company LLC
6 Trowbridge Drive, Suite 5, Bethel, CT 06801-2858, USA
www.crownhousepublishing.com

© Nick Owen 2001

First published 2001; reprinted 2002, 2003 (twice), 2005, 2006, 2007, 2008,
2009 (twice), 2011, 2012.

British Library Cataloguing-in-Publication Data
A catalogue entry for this book is available
from the British Library.

Print ISBN 978-189983670-3
ePub ISBN 978-184590341-1
Mobi ISBN 978-184590215-5
LCCN 2003101973

Printed and bound in the UK by
Bell & Bain Ltd, Glasgow

"Metaphor ... the right brain's unique contribution to the left brain's language capability."

Leonard Shlain
The Alphabet versus the Goddess

"The rational mind is a faithful servant; the intuitive mind a sacred gift.
The paradox of modern life is that we have begun to worship the servant and defile the Divine."

Albert Einstein

"Any sufficiently advanced technology is indistinguishable from magic."

Arthur C. Clarke

"You must be the change you want to see in the world."

Gandhi

For Sofija

Table of Contents

Acknowledgements and Background to the Book

To all the people who asked me where I found the stories and metaphors that I use in my work. Their sheer persistence and refusal to go out and find their own stories encouraged me to start work on my first draft.

The friends and colleagues who not only supported me in embarking on the journey but also gave me their support and valuable feedback at various stages of the project: Joan Albert, Rick Cooper, Helen Eyre, Neil Hutchinson, FCJ, Sofija Mitreva, Dave Pammenter, Rupert Jones Parry, Maire Shelley, and Carolyn Temple.

The many storytellers from whom I have learned much in a variety of different ways. These include Juma Bakari, Paolo Coelho, Judith DeLozier, David Gordon, Noreen Jones, Hugh Lupton, John Morgan, Robert M. Pirsig and Andrew Wright.

Wyatt Woodsmall, who, on a trainer development programme, reconnected me to the teaching device of Master and Apprentice, knower and *ingénu*, a tradition which in recent times includes Antoine de Saint-Exupéry's *Little Prince*, Konstantin Stanislavski's *An Actor Prepares*, Paolo Coelho's *The Pilgrimage*, and Deepak Chopra's *The Way of the Wizard*. The device has proved a particularly useful holding form at various stages of the book.

Few of the stories in the book are my own, so I owe a huge amount of gratitude to storytellers and writers-down-of-stories through the ages who have created, developed, reframed, refined, and passed on so many of these stories. Many of the stories have been handed down from ancient traditions.

I have gathered the stories from a wide variety of sources: during my travels, from friends and acquaintances, at seminars, from books, the movies, the radio, and so on. Although I have reworked and adapted these stories, I have acknowledged, wherever possible, the storyteller or the sources at the end of each story.

I have divided sources into three categories. Primary sources are the people from whom I first heard the story, the book where I first read it, or the medium through which I was first introduced to it. Secondary sources are either the source that my primary source acknowledged, or a reference to books where you can find alternative versions of the story. General sources refer to stories that are widely known and exist in several variations.

Through the agencies of time and familiarity I have forgotten some of my original sources. I would very much welcome reminders from anyone who wishes to set the record straight for future editions.

My own stories have no acknowledgement underneath. Most of these are reflections on events in my own life in different contexts, and I thank those who shared these experiences with me and made them possible. They will recognise their participation when they read the book.

I have learnt much about the power of metaphor applied across a variety of different contexts from Judith DeLozier, Robert Dilts, David Gordon, James Lawley, Penny Tompkins, Julian Russell, Jane Revell, Susan Norman, Christina Hall, John Morgan, Mario Rinvolucri, and Milton Erickson.

I am grateful for the inspiration I have received from authors of other collections of stories, including Rachel Naomi Remen, Clarissa Pinkola Estes, Mario Rinvolucri, John Morgan, Ulli Beier, Jack Canfield, and Mark Victor Hansen.

I have drawn on the wisdom and elegance of stories from Oriental traditions, especially stories from the Sufi tradition. I wish therefore to thank particularly the late Dr. Idries Shah and Dr. Nossrat Peseschkian for their collections of Sufi and Eastern stories (Eastern, of course, only from my perspective). Their scholarship, research, description, and application of stories have been illuminating and inspirational. In collecting and writing down these ancient *teaching* stories they have made possible the dissemination of a treasury of wisdom that the West has long neglected.

These stories have taught me much. And in a very real and humble sense my role as writer and disseminator of the stories in this book is as a conduit to pass on to others the wisdom and variety of the perspectives they offer. My hope is that readers and listeners will continue to learn from them, and in turn pass on their learning to others. This is the *way* of stories.

Information on these writers and their books can be found in the bibliography.

Thanks too to my publishing editor Bridget Shine for her support, enthusiasm, and efficiency, and to Matt Pearce, my editor.

The manuscript was written in London, Hong Kong, New York, Pound Ridge, Skopje, and Sagres. These locations too have been important.

Finally a future thank you to all those of you who select, use, and spread your own interpretations of these stories to a waiting world.

Nick Owen
London
2001

Foreword

Throughout the history of mankind stories have played a part in learning at all levels, from the everyday to the sacred. This has happened because stories teach us through their knots of relevance. It has been my good luck to have been influenced by Milton Erickson and Gregory Bateson. These mentors helped me develop a deeper understanding of connectedness and the ways in which stories serve to promote systemic thinking and systemic living. That's not all. Stories also facilitate problem solving, help us manage transition, and formulate dreams.

Nick has taken a giant step in contributing to our understanding of what a story is. Not only about the story itself, but about the evocative power of the story, and how it is used as a necessary tool of communicating empowerment. Empowerment to the teacher, to the trainer and coach, and empowerment to those who benefit from them.

This comprehensive literature deals with the subject of the story, the role of the trainer as storyteller, and the major tool of a good story: language. Nick has endeavoured to show us that as facilitators, no matter how enthusiastic, charismatic, or skilled with various communication tools we are, we must understand the language of the story.

I myself have been a trainer for 25 years and, like Nick, have found the power of a story one of the most important tools for communicating through a framework that allows the maximum number of participants the possibility to understand a teaching point. This is the quality of a story. It offers a structure that is useful, even though the names and places of the story change.

In fact it has been said[1] that stories serve as models that close the gap between my experience as a human being and the theories I can create to explain my experience. This thought process is referred to as abductive thinking, the thinking which allows us to close the gap between inductive thinking and deductive thinking.

Stories offer the structures that help us go from the specific relata of life to the relationships of life.

From the practical aspect this is a book of stories that enchant us, make us laugh, and help us learn and transform. I thank Nick for making this offering to the world in general and to the trainers of the world specifically. All of this talk about stories reminds me of a story.

A man wanted to know about mind, not in nature, but in his private large computer. He asked it (no doubt in his best Fortran), "Do you compute that you will ever think like a human being?" The machine then set to work to analyse its own computational habits. Finally it printed its answer on a piece of paper, as such machines do. The man ran to get the result and found neatly typed:

That reminds me of a story.

In this little anecdote the suggestion is made that if a computer could truly think like a person it would be able to tell us a story. In other words, the computer could present us with a little knot or complex of that species of connectedness which we call relevance. In this book we find many knots of connectedness that are relevant.

Thanks, you.

Judith DeLozier

---

[1] Gregory Bateson, *Mind and Nature: A Necessity Unity*. London: Fontana. p. 22.

Introduction

Overview

"Why would you be interested in a book of stories?"

The Magician looked at the Young Apprentice and replied: "What is magic?"

"The art of transformation and change."

"Good. And what is the role of a magician?"

"The Magician's role is to assist people to make useful and beneficial changes in their lives."

"And how can this be achieved?"

"By developing greater awareness that all things have a structure, that change is always possible, that there is always more than one perspective, and that the essence of useful change lies in having both creativity and access to a greater number of choices."

"And what is the responsibility of the enlightened Magician?"

The Young Apprentice recalled his studies. "The responsibility of the Magician is to use her power wisely, ethically, and with humility."

"And what are the key principles?"

The Little Magician considered a moment before replying. "There are five key principles.

- A Magician must think systemically and look for the connections between things that are not always apparent. For this reason a Magician must always treat information in its wider context, for nothing exists or makes sense in a vacuum.

- A Magician must always be aware that her knowledge is provisional, that there is always something more to discover, and that there is always more than one way to achieve any outcome.

- A Magician shares her knowledge, for this is an enlightened pathway to empowering others and to achieving immortality.

- A Magician always follows the four Rs: respect for self; respect for others; respect for ecology; and responsibility for all her actions.

- A true Magician believes that none of the above are true, but acts *as if* they are true. She trusts the evidence of her senses to interpret the responses she gets to whatever she does; and she always considers which next choice will be the most appropriate in that particular situation."

"You have learned well," said the Magician. "And these are some of the reasons why a Magician collects and uses stories.

"For all stories are true and yet not true. Every story is complete in its own context, its own reality. Every story therefore reflects a system, a map of the world. Yet just as that map is complete in itself, it is also incomplete because it represents only one among many perspectives.

"Stories offer us a way to see and understand our world in a new light, from a different angle. By challenging our readers and listeners to accept the limitations and shortcomings of their own maps, new insights become possible. Knowing this, you will understand how stories are an important and powerful way to generate creativity and greater choice in our lives. And why Magicians, curious to discover more tools, spend time in bookshops."

About this Book

People often ask, "Where do you find stories?" Stories are everywhere: in books and newspapers, in the movies, in everyday events, in dreams, in the minds and mouths of people, and, above all, in our own lives.

This book is a collection of some of the stories, anecdotes, and extended metaphors that, in my work, I have used in a wide variety of communication contexts. Stories can be used to affirm, change, or challenge people's ideas, attitudes, beliefs, visions, behaviours, skills, and sense of purpose. Contexts in which stories may be applicable are education, business, communication and presentation, health, change work, relationships, the arts, sports, personal development and therapy, and, of course, simply for pleasure.

Resonant stories are essentially reframes. Like putting on different pairs of glasses, stories allow us to look at life and experience in ways that can shift our perspective, range, and focus. Different lenses in the frames allow stories to zoom in, or take a distant view, on their subject. Filters can be attached to a lens to change colour, mood, and energy levels. At their most magical, stories can challenge and disturb our existing frames of reference, our accustomed map of the world, and shift us away from our limited thinking towards new learning and discovery.

The stories that are in this book can be used in a variety of different interpersonal and professional contexts, and they can also be read simply for entertainment.

Framing and Meaning

Without a frame information has no meaning. Consider the following situation. Large black rain clouds have gathered and are now partly obscuring the sun. What is the meaning of this situation? We cannot know until we have understood the context, until we put a *frame* around it.

It could mean a disappointing holiday for a sun worshipper. Or it could mean an excellent time for planting seeds. It might be a disaster for a farmer whose wheat is ripe and ready for harvesting. It might equally be a blessing for a traveller in a waterless desert.

The stories in the book work best when they are told in relation to a particular context. For example, in a situation where a person has moved into a stuck and unresourceful state as a result of a past memory or present experience, the following story might be useful.

Two monks were on a pilgrimage. They had already walked many miles, avoiding where they could the society of people for they were from a particular order of monks that were forbidden to speak to or touch women. They had no wish to offend anyone so they kept to the by-ways and lived off the land.

It was the rainy season and as they walked across a broad plain they were hoping that the river they had to cross would not be impassable. From afar they could see that the river had burst its banks; nevertheless they were hopeful that the ferryman would be able to take them across in his boat. But as they neared the crossing point they could see no sign of the boatman; the boat, it appeared, had been swept away in the current and the ferryman had stayed at home.

There was, however, a woman.

She was dressed in fine clothes and carried an umbrella. She implored the monks to help her cross, for her mission was urgent and the river, though wide and fast, was not deep.

The younger monk ignored her and looked away. The elder, however, said nothing but swept her up onto his shoulder and carried her across, putting her down, completely dry, on the other bank.

For the whole of the following hour as they journeyed on through thick and tangled woods, the younger monk berated the elder, heaping scorn upon his actions, accusing him of betraying the order and his vows. How dare he? How could he? What was he thinking of? What gave him the right to?

Eventually, the monks entered a clearing, and the elder monk stopped and looked square into the eyes of the younger. There was a long moment of silence.

Finally in a soft tone, his eyes bright and gentle with compassion, the older monk simply said: "My brother, I put that woman down an hour ago. It is you that are still carrying her."

The situation of stuckness is the frame that gives the story its power and meaning.

The frame around each of the stories in this book is for you to decide. Stuckness is one of many possible frames for this story. This is a sourcebook of magic, and the meaning of each story will depend on the context in which you tell it, who you are, and who you tell it to.

Meaning and Interpretation

The best stories are multi-layered and capable of rich interpretation. Some stories can contain within them apparently contradictory meanings, such as that entitled "The Quarryman", where it is possible to draw completely opposing conclusions. Depending on personal experience and curiosity, every reader will read different, and sometimes complex, meanings into each story, anecdote, or metaphor.

Perhaps the word metaphor, as used in this book, needs some explanation. I would describe most of the stories in this book as extended metaphors. They are indirect, yet powerful, vehicles for reframing experience from unusual or unexpected perspectives.

Metaphors are not simply poetic or rhetorical embellishments, but powerful devices for shaping perception and experience. If we change the metaphor in which a concept is expressed, we change the frame, making it possible for the concept to be understood differently. It is precisely this change of perspective that allows us greater choice in how we perceive and act upon the world.[1]

Ideas from one set of concepts have been *carried across* or *transferred* (the literal meaning of the Old Greek word *metaphor*) to another set of concepts. This new frame suggests that we reappraise our existing thinking about the original concept. Our ability to *think about* our thinking allows us to take a meta-position

see the original situation with greater perspective, clarity,
om.

One other facet of metaphor that makes it a particularly powerful
tool is that it enables a storyteller to take complex concepts that are
difficult to explain and recreate them in much more concrete
forms. Metaphor allows us to externalise abstract thinking and
translate it into a sensory-based tangible representation. This is
perhaps what Leonard Shlain is referring to in Chapter 1 of his
book *The Alphabet versus the Goddess*,[2] when he writes that
"Metaphor [is] the right brain's unique contribution to the left
brain's language capability."

The power of stories

Every story creates its own highly contextualised world. And
every story combines an inner logic and narrative sequence
expressed through words (left brain preference) together with
aspects of creativity, cohesion, and pattern forming expressed
through tone and emotion (right brain preference). In this way
both hemispheres of our intellectual brain—the neo-cortex—are
stimulated. These factors considerably contribute to our understanding of the following: the attraction of stories as meaning-
carrying vehicles, the memorability of stories, and the appeal of
stories to different ages, cultures, and information-processing
styles.

At a deeper level, stories are archetypes. Stories, metaphors, and
myths carry the history, the culture, the values, and the customs of
the people. They are a form of social glue that serves to entertain,
instruct, and challenge the listener or reader. And because they
strike deep chords in shared communal experience, they operate
at both conscious and unconscious levels, conveying "messages"
directly and indirectly. And it is the connection with the unconscious that challenges and disturbs our comfortable sense of self
and identity, our programmed behaviours, our over habituated
maps of the world. Or, alternatively, confirms them.

Stories also operate through time and space. A biblical parable, a Zen
koan, or a Sufi anecdote can each affect powerfully contemporary

values, behaviours, and contexts. Stories connect the past with the present, and project both past and present into the future.

Connecting between times and contexts, between ideas and concepts, between behaviours and values, stories enable listeners to review and anticipate thought and action. A useful contemporary illustration of this is the TV soap opera. Every episode ends at an unresolved moment of crisis, opening a loop in the viewer's brain. Brains are meaning making organisations and search for completion so that the loop can be closed. The viewer reviews all the information offered in the present and preceding episodes in order to work out possible future outcomes. The soap opera director has created *response-ability*. The heightened anticipation will guarantee the audience for the next episode so the loop can be closed.[3]

In literature, a writer may open up many loops within a story that in a traditional novel will be satisfactorily closed by the denouement. In much contemporary literature the uncertainty principle[4] may be brought into play, so many ways of closing the loops may be offered. Without the closing of loops, however, you don't have a story. Just a sequence of discrete and unrelated facts.[5]

The uses of story

Stories appeal because they connect with readers in so many varied and profound ways. Because they connect at different levels, stories lend themselves to a wide variety of uses. Here are some ways in which stories in this book can be used.

1) Simply for pleasure.
2) Change the mood, state, or energy level of a person or group.
3) Reframe a problem as a new opportunity.
4) See a behaviour or attitude from a different perspective.
5) Disturb a limiting view of the world.
6) Challenge unacceptable behaviour.
7) Offer a model of more useful behaviour or attitude.
8) Teach a point indirectly.
9) Demonstrate that a problem is not new or unique.
10) Enhance creativity.

11) Demonstrate the inadequacies of logical reasoning: a koan.
12) Open a loop, waken the brain, and install information into open minds that are waiting for the loop to be closed.
13) As an overture, introducing key points to be fully dealt with later.
14) As a summary or review of information covered.
15) To search out new possibilities and meanings.
16) To encourage debate and discussion.
17) To challenge or confirm existing world views of listeners.
18) To include the audience in repetitive aspects of the story in order to practise new language structures or vocabulary.
19) To encourage audience involvement and intervention.
20) To encourage story telling among the audience.
21) To develop aspects of presentation skills and public speaking.
22) To introduce aspects of the structure of effective communication.
23) To demonstrate the systemic nature of relationships.
24) To demonstrate how people respond to their map of reality, not reality itself.
25) To fill a gap.
26) To whet a group's appetite. (A lunchtime story)
27) To elicit curiosity.
28) To make a point more memorable.
29) To create powerful associations in listeners' minds.
30) To demonstrate that you want to creatively entertain a group as well as instruct them.
31) To facilitate multi-sensory communication.
32) To surprise people.
33) To include the views and wisdom of other cultures.
34) To demonstrate how the views and wisdom of other cultures have similarities to, and differences from, our own.
35) To induce a light trance state or sleep.
36) To promote and provoke right brain activity.
37) To engage both hemispheres of the upper brain.
38) To shift brain activity from Beta-waves (conscious processing) to Alpha-waves (light trance or day dream state). Alpha-processing is particularly useful for installing

information at a deeper, subconscious level and consolidating material already learned.[6]

39) To install information below the conscious level of awareness.

40) To demonstrate how each person interprets information differently and according to their own unique experience and map of the world.

41) To demonstrate that "perception is projection": our map of the world determines how we will experience the world.

42) To have an excuse to write a book.

43) To have an excuse to read a book.

44) To make connections between past, present, and future.

45) To make the teaching of information more contextualised and memorable.

46) To develop visualisation skills.

47) To make the abstract, concrete.

48) To tap the unconscious mind.

49) To develop an awareness of the sensory basis of language and experience.

50) To develop an appreciation of the role and power of metaphor in stories, and in the communication of meaning in everyday language.

51) To encourage anticipation of the next stage of communication, by finishing the present stage at an uncompleted but critical moment in a story: the Scheherazade Effect.

52) To take a complex idea and "make it as simple as you can, but not any simpler". (Einstein)

53) To challenge complacency.

54) To confirm a cultural viewpoint, attitude, set of values, or beliefs.

55) To shift a paradigm.

56) To create a play.

57) As the basis of a dramatisation.

58) To create cartoons, storyboards, or tableaux (still images).

The Art of Telling Stories

Story telling is an art that lies within the ability of everyone to achieve. To develop the art it is necessary to practise, and to pay attention to feedback. There are four types of feedback. The first is to watch and listen to storytellers that you admire. Ask yourself: *What is it that they are doing that makes such a strong impression on me? How do they do that?* Once you begin to discover what it is that they do, you can begin to model their behaviours. If it works for them, it may well work for you too. This is feedback you give yourself.

The second is feedback others give you while you are telling stories. You will need to maintain eye contact, and keep all your senses open and alert to notice the reactions you are getting as you tell your story. Are they the reactions you want at each stage? Effective story telling is like weaving a spell; you are putting listeners into a light trance, similar to daydreaming, and when you are succeeding it will be easy to move your audience from one state to another. Your feedback here is mainly non-verbal. This does not mean, of course, that your audience is passive. A lot of thinking and emotional processing may be occurring. The more you observe your audience, the more you will know if you are getting the results you want.

The third type of feedback is feedback you give yourself afterwards. What didn't go to plan? What could I have done instead? What other choices were available? What resources do I have that I wasn't using? What difference might each of those resources have made? For example: Was my breathing centred? Did I sufficiently structure my story? Could I have framed it better? Did I choose the right time to tell it?

And when things do go well, congratulate yourself and *also* give yourself feedback. Why was doing *that* so successful? How could I have made it even more effective? Story telling is a journey, and the road to excellence in story telling has no end. You can always get better.

The fourth type of feedback is that which others give you, solicited or unsolicited, after the story telling. It is always worth taking the view that feedback is a gift. At any rate it is not the truth, it is just one person's judgement from their perspective at that particular moment. And you can decide whether to accept it and integrate the feedback into your story telling, think about it, or simply reject it. It is simply information that you can accept or reject.

It can be very useful to invite someone, whose judgement you respect, to sit in on a story and afterwards give you feedback. If you do this, it is best to ask for *specific* feedback on just one or two elements. For example: Was my eye contact evenly spread to all of the audience? Was my voice loud enough? Did I have enough range of emotion or tone? Did I use silences and pauses well? Did my physiology support the different sections of story? Otherwise there is too much information for an observer to notice, and the feedback will tend to be general and of less use.

For a story about feedback and how a champion makes use of it, see the story "Three Steps to Success" [1.08] in the book.

* * *

No excellent storyteller was born an excellent storyteller. It is a learned skill. Earlier in this section the importance of practice was mentioned. But of course there is little point in practising what is not useful. What follows are some practical hints in developing effective story telling skills. Once, through practice, you have become familiar with and mastered these "rules" you can break them. All good rules have a purpose. Once you know the purpose and can achieve it, you can break any rule in the service of a different or higher purpose. The important thing is to know and pursue the purpose. One of the stories in the book to support this view is "The Jar" [1.03].

- Before you start, wherever it is possible, rearrange the furniture to create the best possible relationship between you and your audience, and one which supports the meaning and intention of the story. The *psycho-geography* makes a powerful contribution to how we are affected by the space around us, by the temperature, the lighting, the furniture arrangement, the visual stimuli, and the social relations both within the audience and between audience members and the storyteller.

- Make sure any materials you need, or props, are to hand before starting.

- Before telling a story the first time, rehearse it quietly a couple of times during the previous days using a story skeleton (see below). Just before telling it publicly, run a quick movie of it in your head.

- Take time to compose yourself before you start. Aim to put yourself in a state that matches the mood you want at the opening of your story. If you want calm, think of a time, any time, when you had that kind of calm. It can be in any context, provided it was a time of calm. As you connect with that memory, take time to see the pictures of the memory, and hear the sounds of the memory. The sights and sounds will trigger the feelings of the calm you had then, right now in the present. Practise this so that just a quick thought of what you saw or heard brings back the feeling instantly. Of course, you can use the same technique with excitement, curiosity, energy, anticipation, or any other emotional state. This is a technique many top performers use in business, the arts, and sport.

- Finally, before beginning, develop a centred breathing pattern, right down into your belly, while maintaining a relaxed sense of wellbeing in your shoulders and upper chest. Breath is the centre of life and also of your voice. You will have access to greater vocal and emotional range when you are breathing well. It will also slow you down and give you a sense of rootedness and control.

- Mark the transition from the previous activity into a story with a moment of silence and inclusive eye contact. A story needs ritual and it is important that listeners appreciate that a change of context is imminent, that something is about to begin. Aim for a frisson of tension like that before the start of a Grand Prix, or the curtain rising in the theatre, or a space rocket taking off. The excitement and anticipation is in those moments before the activity starts.

- Where possible tell a story rather than read it. An effective storyteller brings life to a story through her own identification with it. Reading a story well is a much more challenging skill because it requires you to interpret someone else's story rather than your own personal version of it.

● An excellent way to make a story your own is to create a skeleton of the original story and use it as the basis of your own interpretation. Here's an example based on the story of the two monks, used earlier in the introduction.

> Two monks
> Women: no talk/touch
> Rainy season
> Flooded river
> Woman
> Older monk—carries her
> Younger—betrayed
> One hour non-stop
> Finally
> I… You…

With a couple of rehearsals your brain needs nothing more than this to trigger the memory and structure the story. Probably, the emotional and intellectual process of selecting which words to use in your skeleton will be enough to fix the story firmly in your memory. Do not be tempted to put too much information into the skeleton. When telling the story the first few times, you can have this skeleton by you on an unobtrusive record card, or write it large in big bold letters and put it on the wall behind your audience, where you can see it easily, keeping your eye contact outwards, not down.

● If you have only this skeleton you will have to trust yourself to find the linking ideas and words *fresh each time* you tell the story. It will then be *in your own words*. This will ensure your story is full of vitality. You will be searching for the words and ideas, and the searching will slow you down. As if you are crossing a river on stepping stones, your delivery will be full of changes of direction and moments of drama. You will make natural pause breaks for thought, and you will now have time to connect to the reality and emotions of your story through visual, auditory, and emotional processing.

- Slow down. You will have to speak slower than natural talking speed, and for some of you this will feel uncomfortable. There are several reasons why slower than normal speed is desirable. Unlike reading, where you can go at your own speed, and re-read a paragraph if you don't understand it, listeners have to process at the speed of the speaker. In our stories we want our listeners to paint pictures in their mind's eye, to hear the voices of our characters in their mind's ear, to connect with their inner emotions as each narrative progresses from section to section. And for this they need time. The time you offer your listeners, through silence, pause, and pace allows them to think back over what has been said and connect it with their own past experience, to consider how they are feeling about it now in the present, and to anticipate the future, what will happen next. And so you bind a greater and deeper connection between you, the teller, and them, the listeners.

- Choose stories that are meaningful to you so that the reality of each story, and your emotional contact with it, naturally allow you to use the tonalities of your voice, its energy and range, which are appropriate to each part of the story. The same is true for volume and pace. This will tend to occur naturally as you *experience* the story as you tell it.

- Maintain eye contact with all your audience, sometimes sweeping across the whole of the audience, sometimes holding eye contact with an individual for three to five seconds. This connects you with the listeners and gives you feedback about how you are doing. With eye contact in groups, less than three seconds with one particular individual is often not noticed. More than five seconds can be an embarrassment.

- Pay attention to the state you want to put your audience in. Will the story excite them or calm them, make them curious, or challenge them? Or all of these at different stages of the story? What is the purpose of your story at an individual, social, cultural, educational, and political level? When you are clear about the purpose of your story, you are more likely to achieve the results you want.

- Look for stories in newspapers, books, TV, radio and movies, and especially in anecdotes from your own life. Experiment with telling the same story in different ways, and making changes in a story to achieve different results and responses.

- Always bear in mind that the power of effective story telling depends on several key factors. First, the frame you put around each story. Second, your willingness to withhold your own interpretation so that others can freely supply theirs. Third, your commitment to, and involvement in, the telling. Fourth, that the meaning of any story depends upon the context in which you tell it, who you are, and who you tell it to.

For another perspective on preparation for story telling, you might like to take a look at the story entitled "The Warrior of the Shadows" [1.13].

Organisation and style

The Apprentice asked the Master, "Why have the stories in the book not been rigorously categorised and interpreted?"

The Magician replied, "At this I can only guess. However, if I were to put myself in the shoes of the writer, my own thinking would be like this.

"First, to categorise is to label. And labelling, while useful, can often be limiting. Categorising might suggest that such and such a story has a particular meaning, or there is a particular way of interpreting it."

"Can you give me an example?" asked the Little One.

"Well, take, for example, the story called 'The Quarryman' [2.04]. What are we to make of it? Is it a story about being content with one's situation in life and not complaining? Or is it about striving to achieve more than one dreams is possible? Is it about destiny? Or does it tell us about change, flexibility, and the need to set goals? Is it concerned with domestication or liberation, as the

Wizard Paolo Freire[7] might ask? Or are we to think that everything in the world is divinely ordered? Or is it a story about systems thinking or chaos theory? ..."

"OK! OK!" said the Young Apprentice, seeing his Master was going to continue with her list of possible interpretations. "I see what you mean. What are the other reasons?"

"Secondly, part of the pleasure of reading is not to look for particular prefigured solutions but to be surprised by the possible interpretations that arise from the interaction between the words on the page and one's own experience and knowledge."

"Ah yes! That's exactly what the Chinese professor says in the story called 'The Jar' [1.03]."

"Precisely so," said the Wise One. "Third, had I written these stories, or written them down from other sources, I myself would not have an idea how to categorise them. For I myself can see so many possible interpretations in each of the stories. I would have to put some stories in many different categories for I would not wish to choose one above another."

"Yes, I begin to understand," said the Little Magician. "So what's to be done?"

"Well, as you can see, the collection is not haphazard. The stories are grouped loosely around similarities, themes, and sources."

"Is that a solution?"

"It is certainly *a* solution. Whether it is the best is a matter of opinion. At the end of the day, the meaning of any message is the response it gets. And no doubt many readers will make their own groupings according to their personal interpretations. And that is just as it should be. Besides, as I have said many times, it is more the context in which a story is told, the frame that is put around it, and the relationship between teller and audience, which really provide the meaning of a story."

"And," said the Young One, "who is to say that every individual in the audience understands it in the same way as the teller? Or as each other?"

"Very true. You have spoken well."

"I'm also curious about style. It seems there are different styles of story in this collection."

"That is true," said the Magician. "Some are fully worked out, while others are sparse and spare. Some are quite long, while others are no more than a couple of lines."

"Why do you think that is?" the Little Magician inquired.

"Perhaps, for who am I to divine the mind of another, it is to show that there are many kinds of story, that they are plentiful and always available to us. Something one person finds commonplace and ordinary; another can find something useful in it and turn it into a story. Often a few words, well chosen and at the right time, are enough. There is no correct way for a story to be, any more than there is a right way to tell it."

"So the message is," said the Little Magician, "take these stories and make them your own."

"Precisely. Feel free to change and adapt them to suit you, your context, and the needs of your audience. And, above all, have fun with them because they are a celebration of the richness and diversity of life of which each of us is part."

"And are these stories original?"

"A few are original, but many of them I have heard or read before. The important thing is that here they have been re-told and reworked in a unique and original way. So they add a different dimension and perspective to previous interpretations."

"But is it right," asked the Young Apprentice, "to change somebody else's story?"

"It depends. There are professional storytellers who travel the world listening to and collecting stories and remembering them so they are preserved for future generations. This is an important contribution. And all storytellers recognise their debt to the one they first heard the story from, knowing that that storyteller holds a debt to the one they first heard the story from, knowing that that storyteller holds …"

"So in many ways stories go back to the beginning of the world?"

"I remember," said the Magician, "a professional storyteller, Hugh Lupton of Norfolk, finishing one of his excellent stories, and saying something like:

> 'Jack Maguire of Donegal told me that story
> And as I tell the story
> I can feel Jack's ghost standing right behind me
> And behind him, the one who told him the story
> And behind her the one who told her the story
> Stretching way back to the beginning of time
> Each one listening to the telling of his story
> In a different mouth
> One behind the other in long line of creative ancestry
> And every time I make the smallest change
> In the story he told me
> I feel Jack give me a sharp dig in the ribs
> To remind me
> That I've strayed from the one true telling'

"But, you know," said the Magician, "I know that Jack had plenty of digs in the ribs himself, and the one before, and the one before that. And as well as a dig in the ribs, I reckon there was also a secret admiration for a new creative possibility, and sometimes just a hint of: 'I wish I'd thought of that meself.' A dig in the ribs and a creative caress at one and the same time."

"So I understand," said the Little Magician, "I am to respect the past, and use it wisely in the present to shape the new. Connecting between what is gone and what is to come, and in applying my own creativity, according to the needs of the moment, to celebrate my own power to act upon the world."

"My young friend, you are already a Magician."

[1] For a fuller discussion of this see: Lakoff, George & Johnson, Mark. *Metaphors We Live By*. Chicago: University of Chicago Press, 1980.

[2] Shlain, Leonard. *The Alphabet versus the Goddess*. London: Penguin Arkana, 2000.

[3] The brain tends to remember incomplete information better than completed information when the message is interrupted at a critical point. This is known as the Zeigarnick or Scheherazade effect. A good example is the technique commonly used at the end of each episode of a television soap opera.

[4] *The Uncertainty Principle*: Werner Heisenberg's contribution to quantum physics and a forerunner of chaos theory and fuzzy logic. For an excellent example of the uncertainty principle in literary practice see Michael Frayn's play *Copenhagen*.

[5] For a more fully worked out description of this see: Keith Johnstone. *Improvisation*. London: Methuen, 1981: 109ff.

[6] For more on brain patterns see: Rose, Colin & Nicoll, Malcolm. *Accelerated Learning for the 21st Century*. London: Piatkus, 1997.

[7] Freire, Paulo. *Pedagogy of the Oppressed*. London: Continuum, 1992.

Section 1

Pacing and Leading

Pacing and Leading

"I know what leading is," said the Young Apprentice, "but what exactly is pacing?"

"Pacing, in this context, means walking in step with another person or group of people. But do not be misled by the apparent simplicity of this explanation. Pay attention to the metaphorical power of being in step with other people in the context of communicating with them. What could it mean?"

The Apprentice reflected for a moment or two. "I suppose it could mean tailoring your communication to fit initially with another person's model of reality."

"Meaning what specifically?"

"Well, for example, if my friend was upset by something that had happened to him, I would share his sense of upset-ness to let him know I care about how he feels. Having done this, and given him my support, I can then gently move him towards feeling more positive and resourceful. Perhaps, once he understands that I care about and respect his feelings, and that I accept the way he responds to events in his life, he might be more willing to listen to my suggestion of going to a movie or something else. And in this way he may begin to change his upset state to a more useful one where he can do something about the cause of the upset."

"Excellent," said the Magician. "So what sort of things could you pace in a more formal context such as managing a meeting, giving a presentation, conducting an interview, teaching a class, going out on a date?"

"Well, I guess I could initially pace the energy or mood of the person or group, or their level of knowledge, or understanding of a topic, or the things they are interested in, or the skills they have or lack, or their values and beliefs. There are lots of ways I could begin a communication that lets others know that I am curious about, interested in, and respect where they are coming from."

"Precisely. Pacing is the art of building a relationship or rapport with a person or a group of people. And without this art you will find it very hard to be an effective leader. Effective leaders understand that if they want others to follow them in a common or shared purpose, they must first build a respectful and trusting relationship to establish channels of communication through which information can flow."

The Young One said, "I'm not sure I see exactly what you mean."

The Magician replied, "Let me draw you a map."

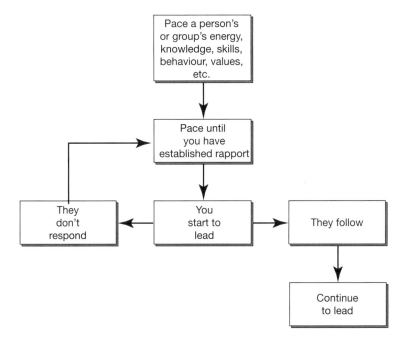

"The test for rapport is very simple," said the Magician. "When you start to lead, others will want to follow.

"The stories in this section of the book have been chosen to build a relationship with the readers, and also to allow readers to use the stories to build relationships with other people in a variety of wide-ranging contexts. If that rapport is built, it will then be possible to lead others into experiencing the way they understand reality from new perspectives, to see the world through different frames, and to encourage others to do the same."

"And is that all these stories do?" asked the Little One.

"All these stories are rich and complex, some more than others, and are open to a wide range of meanings. Only the reader can decide what each story specifically or generally means for his or her own self and how, when, and where they might want to use it for themselves or with others ... now ... are you sitting comfortably? Then we'll ..."

1.01   Core Learning (Taking the Pith)

An Apprentice complained to a Magician, "You tell us stories but don't explain what they mean."

The Magician replied, "And when you go to the fruit shop to buy oranges, do you ask the greengrocer to taste it for you, leaving you with just the skin?"

General source: Sufi tradition.

1.02   *The Book of Stories*

The Apprentice Magician said, "I have written a book of stories containing *joie de vivre*, insight, and provocation. Even if the price were a hundred gold pounds, those who recognise the potential of these stories, and the infinite variety of their uses, would say the price is cheap."

The Magician, his master, replied, "I shall write a book that offers the key to interpreting and understanding each and every one of your stories. Yet even though I offer it for free, few will trouble to read a book that offers wisdom, erudition, and knowledge."

The Apprentice Magician countered, "I am assuming that those who read this book have all the resources they need to work out, in their own ways and for each specific context, their own interpretations for themselves. For who can say what a story means except the person who reads it on the basis of her own knowledge and experience?"

The Magician said, "I am a Magician, and you are my Apprentice. You are also a Magician, and I am also your Apprentice. The candle is not there to illuminate itself."

The Apprentice became silent and began to consider what the Magician might have meant by that.

General source: Various traditions.

1.03   *The Jar*

The very famous Chinese professor from the very famous Chinese university sat in front of a group of new students. In front of him was a large glass jar, translucent and slightly greenish. The kind of jar some people keep plants in.

The professor looked at the students but said nothing. Then he leaned down to his right hand side. By his foot was a pile of fist-sized rocks. He took a rock and very carefully dropped it through the hole at the top of the neck of the jar. Then another and another and another. Until no more rocks could be dropped through the hole at the top of the neck of the jar.

He turned to the group and said: "Tell me, is the jar now full?"

The group murmured assent: the jar was now full.

The professor said nothing and turned to his left side. By his foot was a pile of pebbles. He took a handful of pebbles and carefully poured them through the hole at the top of the neck of the jar. Handful by handful, around the rocks, until no more pebbles could be poured through the hole at the top of the neck of the jar.

He turned to the group and said: "Tell me, is the jar now full?"

The group mumbled that it certainly appeared as if the jar could possibly now be full, maybe.

The professor said nothing and turned again to his right side. By his foot was a pile of coarse dry sand. He took a handful of sand and carefully poured it through the hole at the top of the neck of the jar. Around the rocks, around the pebbles, handful by handful, until no more sand could be poured through the hole at the top of the neck of the jar.

He turned to the group and said: "Tell me, is the jar now full?"

There was silence.

The professor said nothing and turned again to his left side. By his foot was a jug of water. He took the jug and carefully poured the water through the hole at the top of the neck of the jar. Around the rocks, the pebbles, the sand. Until no more water could be poured through the hole at the top of the neck of the jar.

He turned to the group and said: "Tell me, is the jar now full?"

There was silence, even more profound than before. The kind of silence where those present check to see if their nails are clean or their shoes polished. Or both.

The professor turned again to his right side. On a small blue square of paper he had a small pile of fine dry salt. He took a fingerful of salt and carefully dissolved it in the water at the top of the neck of the jar. Fingerful by fingerful in the water, around the sand, around the pebbles, around the rocks, until no more salt could be dissolved in the water at the top of the neck of the jar.

Once again the professor turned to the group and said: "Tell me, is the jar now full?"

One very courageous student stood up and said: "No, Professor, it is not yet full."

The professor said: "Aaah! But it *is* now full."

The professor then invited all the people who were there to consider the meaning of his story. What did it mean? How did they interpret it? Why had the professor told it? And after some minutes the professor listened to their reflections.

There were as many interpretations as there were people in the room.

When the professor had heard from each of the students, he congratulated them, saying that it was hardly surprising there were so many different interpretations. After all, everybody there was a unique individual who had lived through unique experiences, unlike those of anybody else. Their interpretations simply

9

reflected their own lived experience and the particular and unique perspective through which they understood the world.

And in that sense no interpretation was any better, or any worse, than any other. And, he wondered, were the group curious to know his own interpretation? Which of course, he stated, was no better or worse than theirs. It was simply his interpretation.

Oh yes, they were curious.

"Well," he said, "my interpretation is simply this. Whatever you do in life, whatever the context, just make sure you get your rocks in first."

Primary source: Julian Russell.
There are many versions of this story.

1.04   The Door

A captain of industry was looking for an able and wise manager who would have the skills and acuity to take over the running of the organisation after he had retired. He assembled the best managers from his own company and hired recruitment consultants and headhunters to find him additional ones who might serve his purpose.

On a particular day, all the possible contenders were assembled in a great hall of a mighty palace, which the organisation had hired for that day.

The captain of industry addressed the assembled hand-picked managers. "I have a problem, and I want to know who among you has the wherewithal to solve it. What you see in the wall behind me is the biggest, mightiest, and heaviest door in the kingdom. Who among you, without assistance, has the power to open it?"

Some of the managers simply shook their heads. It was just too big a problem. Others examined the door more closely, discussed aspects of leverage and mass, remembered theories of problem solving they had learned in business school, and admitted that it seemed to be an impossible task.

When the wisest and most respected had accepted defeat, all the others capitulated too.

Only one manager approached the door and gave it a thorough close up examination. He tapped it, assessed its width and depth, noticed the nature and lubrication of its hinges. He checked it thoroughly with his eyes and hands. Prodding here, pushing here, poking there. Finally he made his decision. He breathed deeply, centred himself, and pulled gently on the door.

It swung open easily and effortlessly.

The others had made the assumption that the door had been locked or jammed. In fact it had been left ever so slightly ajar and the carpentry and design were so excellent only the slightest touch was required to open it.

The captain of industry had his successor. He addressed the managers assembled there. "Success in life and industry depends on certain key things. They are these as we have just seen demonstrated. First, rely on your senses to fully understand the reality of what is going on around you. Second, do not make false assumptions. Third, be willing to make tough decisions. Fourth, have the courage to act with boldness and conviction. Fifth, put your powers into action. Finally, do not be afraid to make mistakes."

General source: Oriental tradition.

1.05   *Gandhi's Completeness*

The story goes that on a certain day Gandhi and a companion entered the gates of a great city in order to share their teachings with the inhabitants. Almost immediately a follower of the Mahatma, who lived in the city, approached and told him, "Master, you are wasting your time and energy here. The people here are hard of heart, and resistant to change and the words of truth. They are dumb and ignorant and have no wish to learn anything. Do not waste your gifts upon them."

Gandhi smiled at the man and replied, "I have no doubt you are right."

Some minutes later another adherent approached Gandhi saying, "My Lord, you are indeed most welcome by all in this fortunate city. The people await and anticipate the jewels of learning that will fall from your lips. They are hungry to learn and eager to serve you. Their hearts and minds are truly open to you."

Gandhi smiled and replied, "I have no doubt you are right too."

His companion turned to him and said, "Master, how is it possible you can say one thing to one man and something completely different to another? The sun and the moon can never be the same thing, and day cannot be night."

Gandhi smiled at his friend and replied, "I have no doubt you are right. And you may also consider that both men spoke truly according to their own values. The first expects to see the bad in everything. The second sees only the good. Both men perceive the world as they expect it to be. How can you say either man perceives wrongly since all humankind perceives the world as they choose to experience it? Neither man spoke falsely; just something incomplete."

General source: There are similar stories in various traditions.
I don't recall who first told me this as a Gandhi story.

1.06a On Message

At a political rally a supporter asked Gandhi: "Mahatma, I am a simple man and do not understand many things, so tell me simply, what is your message?"

Gandhi looked at the man for a moment before replying, "I am my message."

Primary source: Anecdotal.

1.06b Walking the Talk

One time, a woman came to Gandhi and asked him to tell her overweight son to stop eating sugar.

"Madam," he replied, "come back in three weeks' time."

Surprised at this request, she nevertheless returned with her son three weeks later.

Gandhi looked at the boy and said, "Stop eating sugar."

When the boy had left the room, the mother turned to Gandhi and asked why he hadn't said this three weeks ago.

Gandhi replied, "Madam, three weeks ago I myself was eating sugar."

Primary source: Christina Hall.

1.07   *Einstein and Intelligence*

Einstein was once asked what he considered the main difference between his own intelligence and that of other people. He thought for a while, and replied: "Well, when most people look for a needle in a haystack, they stop when they find it. But I will continue looking to discover if I can find a second, a third, and maybe, if I am very lucky, a fourth or fifth needle."

Primary source: Albert McMahon.

1.08   *Three Steps to Success*

The former world tennis champion was being interviewed on a radio programme. "Had he always been a champion?" the interviewer asked.

No, he hadn't, he said. Although when he'd been young he'd been picked as a potential future prospect. But other boys had been better than him, more naturally gifted. And he had often had to play the best of the girls, who were a better match for him than the more naturally talented boys.

"So where are they now, these boys?" said the interviewer. "What happened to them all?"

"Well," said the former champion, "they just didn't make it. For all their talent they didn't have what it takes."

"So what does it take?" asked the interviewer.

"You've got to want it enough."

"Is that the secret?"

"There's another. It takes discipline. No matter how much talent you have, you've got to have the discipline to nurture and develop it. You've got to prioritise and give up a lot of things that can seem very attractive at the time."

"Is that the secret?"

"There's another," said the former tennis ace, "and it's harder and more demanding than the first two put together. You need humility, no matter how good you are. You need humility to listen to your coaches, to take advice, to test new possibilities, and to admit you don't know everything. Feedback is the breakfast of champions. These three things are the secrets of my success."

Primary source: A delegate on a training course told me about this (reconstructed) sports radio interview with Boris Becker.

1.09   *Vision*

There was a certain great entrepreneur, a man who had envisioned and brought to profitable fruition many great enterprises, who had brought employment to many people around the globe, and who was widely praised for his sense of purpose, decision making, and fair play.

One day his personal assistant came to him with a grim expression on his face.

"Why the long face?" asked the entrepreneur.

"I am angry at the stupidity of people and their ingratitude. You are the most reasonable, wisest, and most talented of leaders. You are also the most powerful. You make whatever decision you wish, and others must obey. And yet what do I hear as I pass through the corridors of your offices and factories as I travel round the world? Of course, there are many who praise you; but there are also many who speak ill of you. They criticise your decisions, they question your honesty, they laugh at your stutter, they ridicule your dreams. How is it that such ingratitude can be found in those who owe you so much?"

The entrepreneur smiled and replied, "Just as everybody else in our great enterprise, you know well what I have achieved for you all. From humble beginnings, our enterprise now offers work and prosperity to tens of thousands of people across five continents. Our products are produced with commitment and quality, and are of value to those who buy and use them. For all this, I am ultimately responsible. Those who work in our organisation respect me for the opportunities I have brought them, for my sense of justice and fair play, for the progress I have brought them, their families, and their communities. I have the power to close factories and offices, to seal them up, and to create misery where there has been only progress.

"But there is one thing I cannot do. I cannot shut the mouths of my employees. However, it is not important that some people speak ill of me. What is important is that I do what I can to serve them, to serve the community in which we all live, and to serve the dream that drives me to do all this."

Primary source: Nossrat Peseschkian, Oriental Stories as Tools in Psychotherapy. See bibliography.
General source: Oriental tradition.

1.10   Leadership

The Apprentice just managed to arrive in time for the class. His cheeks were flushed from running and his heart was pumping hard. The topic was *Influential Leadership.*

The Apprentice asked, "What is leadership?"

The Magician replied, "The question is rather, *'How do you lead yourself?'*"

"I don't understand. What do you mean?"

"For example, how did you get yourself out of bed this morning? Did you force yourself out unwillingly, fearing the consequences of being late for my class? Or did you spring easily out of bed, saying, *'The day deserves me!'*"

"Hmmmpph!"

"Only when you know how to lead yourself influentially will you then know how to lead others."

1.11   *Prayers for the Sole*

A worshipper was praying at a holy shrine. He was wearing a most beautiful pair of soft leather slippers, stitched with great skill, designed with stylish elegance, and dyed with artful brilliance.

A fellow worshipper noticed the quality of these slippers and was struck by their attractiveness. He gently leaned across to the worshipper who owned the beautiful shoes and in a soft, beguiling voice said, "Are you not aware, my friend, that prayers prayed with shoes on never reach God's ears?"

The beautifully shod worshipper paused for a moment in his prayers and replied in an equally silky voice, "Then at least if God does not hear my prayers, I will still have my slippers."

Primary source: Nossrat Peseschkian.
General source: Oriental tradition.

1.12   Being on Top

A merchant, a staunch pillar of society, wanted to protect his daughter from shame. When he realised she had become a ripe and succulent apple, ready for plucking, he took her aside one day and said, "My daughter, wicked and slippery are the ways of men in this world, and you must exercise the greatest care if you are not to bring disgrace on yourself and your family."

Now that he had his daughter's attention, he continued, "Men are after only one thing, are exceedingly devious, and will stop at nothing to fulfil their lustful desires. I want only to keep you from harm and disgrace. So listen carefully to what I am going to tell you, so you will know how to protect yourself when the time comes.

"At first a man will admire and praise your beauty and charms. Then he will flatter you, and invite you to spend time with him. The next thing is that he will walk you by his house, as if by chance, and remember he has something important inside that he needs to fetch. And of course he will invite you to come in while he looks for it.

"While you are waiting he will offer you a seat and, as if out of politeness, something to drink in order to refresh yourself. Now he sits down next to you, and you listen to music together. And when the moment is right, he makes his move. He forces himself on top of you, and in this way are you violated, you and your family shamed, and our reputation ruined."

The daughter was much impressed by this forceful and passionate speech of her father. She took serious notice of it and resolved never to bring shame upon herself or her family.

Some time later she approached her father with reverence. "Are you a magician?" she inquired. "Everything was just as you predicted. First he admired me, then he invited me out. Next the dear boy took me by his house from which he needed something from his bedside cupboard. Of course he invited me inside so I wouldn't have to wait outside alone, and once inside his apartment he offered me a drink, just as you had said. Then we listened to some soothing, relaxing music.

"But all this time I remembered your words, and I knew exactly what was about to happen. So let me tell you how I am worthy to be your daughter. Just when I felt the right moment coming and he was about to make his move, I forced myself on top of him, and in this way violated him, shamed him and his family, and ruined *their* reputation."

Primary source: Mariel Gonzales.
Secondary source: Nossrat Peseschkian.
General source: Oriental tradition.

1.13   The Warrior of the Shadows

The Apprentice Magician had almost reached the end of his training. Soon he would be travelling the paths of the world, sharing his knowledge and gifts with all who cared to learn the secrets of life. He began to feel the seeds of a deep discomfort stir within him.

He approached his Master and asked, "Master, soon I will have to communicate the learning you have given to me to other people. Sometimes to large groups, sometimes to just one person. What are the secrets of successful communication? What are the most effective ways to present my ideas to other people?"

"Wake up!" replied the Master not unkindly. "You already know these things for yourself. If you can recognise the difference between an excellent communicator and a poor one, you have the tools to work out what each is doing to achieve the results they are getting."

"Master, I understand that I already know many things. I know that by discovering the qualities I have that match those of presenters I admire I will be able to reinforce my existing skills. And I also know that the external world also exists to serve me if only I will pay sufficient attention to what it is telling me. You yourself are accomplished as a communicator. What can I learn of presentation from you?"

The Master thought for a moment. "As a prelude to your next area of study, consider this. First, that the nervousness you are already feeling, the butterflies in your stomach, is a good sign. They show that you care, and caring is the essential ingredient of quality. You care about yourself, you wish to be the best you can. You care about your audience, you want them to understand, appreciate, enjoy, and know how to apply what you are sharing with them. Lastly, you care about your material, what it contains, and how it is structured. You believe it is important; it is important for you, and will be important for them when you put it across in ways that are appropriate for them."

"But what can I do about the butterflies?"

The Master permitted herself a wry smile. "Perhaps you should learn the ancient Eastern art of stage flight."

"What is stage flight, Master?"

"Stage flight," said the Master with smiling eyes, "is the art of making the butterflies fly in formation."

The Master paused, allowing time for the Young Apprentice to appreciate the humour and connect the visual image with his inner emotions. Then she continued. "There are many aspects that make up the great arts of successful communication and effective presentation. The next stage in your apprenticeship is to learn the arts of self-preparation and self-control. For if you are not centred in yourself, and with your material, you will lack the edge you seek. And for this you must study with the Warrior of the Shadows, the Master who taught your Master."

"And where will I find the Warrior of the Shadows?" inquired the Young One. "At the place where you might most expect to meet him," replied the Magician.

And so it was that later in the day the Apprentice Magician set off on the long journey to the place where the sun sets between the mountains, the place where the shadows are longest and deepest. He travelled for three days across broad plains, over ranging hills, through dark valleys, over deep rivers, until he arrived at the cleft in the mountains where the sun sets, and among the rocks he waited.

The Apprentice Magician waited and watched long into the night until sleep overcame him. He awoke early in the morning with the sun in his eyes, an ache in his back, and a pair of deep blue eyes penetrating deep into his soul.

"Wake up!" said the Warrior of the Shadows. "A Magician, even an Apprentice, should never be unprepared."

"My Master sent me," blurted out the Young One. "She said you would teach me how to prepare myself for presentation and communication."

"I cannot teach you anything," replied the Warrior gruffly. "Learning, on the other hand, is another matter. Learning is your responsibility. It will happen when you are ready for it. Are you ready?"

"I am, for most certainly I want to learn these things."

"Then you will indeed learn, provided you pay close enough attention. Stay where you are. Keep quiet and watch with full attention."

Before the Young Apprentice could think of something to say the Warrior of the Shadows was moving away among the rocks. He moved silently between the outcrops and open spaces, intently scanning the terrain. He examined the nature of each space and how it related to other spaces; he noted the places where access and movement were easy and where they were difficult. Finally he appeared to make a decision, for he ceased pacing and scanning the space he was in and stopped still.

It seemed to the Apprentice as he watched that the Warrior of the Shadows became as one with the space he was in. The Warrior's breathing shifted to a place deep within the centre of himself, his upper body was motionless, and all that could be seen was a deep rise and fall in the area of his belly. Yet the breath seemed to fill the whole space he was in, and the Warrior's presence seemed to make an impact even upon the rocks that walled in the open space he occupied.

After some moments in which, as it seemed to the Apprentice Magician, the Warrior of the Shadows was completely still yet filling the whole space, the Warrior moved suddenly and with purpose. He removed the pack that was slung across his back which was carrying his few belongings, and placed it carefully under an overhanging rock. He took from his pockets several pouches, artefacts, and other objects, and placed them carefully out of sight with the backpack. He removed his outer coat and the Young Apprentice saw for the first time the Warrior's long elegant fighting stick gleaming dully in the early sunlight.

And only then did the Little Apprentice become aware of the danger the Warrior of the Shadows was in. From every angle the enemy was approaching. Shadow Warriors, sixteen in total, their swords drawn, their hostile intention against the Warrior of the Shadows expressed clearly in their eyes and in every movement.

The songs of the birds stopped, and the chorus of the grasshoppers fell silent. A quiet tension hung over the battleground. The Warrior of the Shadows appeared attentive yet totally unconcerned. It seemed to the Little Magician as he crouched even lower in his hiding place that another transformation took place. Standing in the centre of his chosen space, the Warrior of the Shadows stood completely still. Relaxed, flowing, yet completely still; his breathing deep and centred. He raised his fighting hand high above his head and, as if plucking something down from the sky, he slowly let his hand drop across his face, his breast, his stomach, until it rested at a point three fingers below his navel.

His breathing deepened, he seemed to grow in stature, and vibrate with a powerful energy. To the Young Magician it seemed as if the Warrior of the Shadows was transformed into something magnificent and untouchable. Indeed it seemed as if he was floating above the earth.

At this moment the sixteen warriors charged. Their weapons were drawn and their shouts filled the air. And yet the Warrior of the Shadows still had time to pause. He smiled, bent down, and from a small crevice among the stones beneath his feet he plucked a tiny scarlet flower. He took time to notice its elegant structure, the brilliance of its colour, and to savour its delicate aroma even as the enemy bore down upon him. It was as if, for an instant, time stood still and all energy was focused in one quiet place deep within him. And then …

Suddenly, in the time it took for the first enemy's sword to strike down towards his skull, the Warrior of the Shadows was gone from that space, dancing lightly on the balls of his feet, his stick shimmering. Air, stick, sword, blood blurred to the Young Apprentice's sight, crowns cracked, ribs wrecked, collars cut, necks gashed and, as it seemed to the Young One, the Warrior of the Shadows moved with the speed of lightning and the grace and ferocity of a panther. Seemingly slow yet deceptively fast, the Warrior of the Shadows appeared to have all the time in the world. And by now the enemy were fleeing in confusion, their attack thwarted, sixteen beaten Shadow Warriors melting silently back into the shadows from where they had come.

The Warrior of the Shadows collected his belongings and nonchalantly walked across to where the Little Apprentice was still collecting his breath and thoughts.

"So if you are ready, tell me what you learned," said the Warrior. "Are you ready to understand the structure of true warriorship?"

The Little Apprentice gathered his thoughts. He took a deep breath, remembering the trick of breathing down to the centre of his being, about three fingers below his navel and two fingers in.

"As I watched it seemed to me that the first thing you did was to search out a space that was suitable for you. You chose a place where you would have the advantage, in which you could move around in comfort and ease, and which would suit the purpose and style of the engagement you had in mind."

"Very good," said the Warrior of the Shadows. "Choose your territory. This is the first rule of engagement."

"Then, you paused and changed your breathing pattern. You became calm and still, and it seemed as if your presence and breath filled the whole space you had chosen."

"You have observed well. Take time to centre yourself. This is the second rule of engagement."

"You then took off your backpack, emptied your pockets, and removed everything from the arena that would not serve you."

"Correct. Discard all unnecessary things. This is the third rule of engagement."

"The next thing I noticed was that you reached up and appeared to pull down something out of the sky and connect it to something in the very deepest part of you."

"Indeed. Connect to a Higher Power. The Breath of Life resides in our *inspiration*. This is the fourth rule of engagement."

"Then you did something really surprising. Even as all the enemy were rushing towards you, as if you cared nothing about this, you bent down, picked a flower, and took time to fully experience its beauty."

"Excellent. Before engagement, free yourself from conscious thoughts for in moments of crisis your mind won't help. This is the fifth rule of engagement."

The Young Apprentice looked a little puzzled. The Warrior of the Shadows read his mind: "If you are not fully prepared before engagement begins, you will be unable to *respond in the moment with the full array of your resources*. Successful improvisation requires pattern and structure."

The Apprentice nodded thoughtfully before getting back to the action. "And then in an instant you were present again and instantly moving. And it seemed to me that you were able to move twice as fast as each of your enemies and yet you appeared to have twice as much time to think, decide, and strike."

"This is the sixth and last rule of engagement," said the Warrior of the Shadows. "You must learn to slow down time. And once you have learned to do that you will also know how to move and think faster in any moment of crisis or danger. And you will also learn to savour better those moments of sweet pleasure."

"But how do I learn to slow down time? How is that possible?"

"The answer is as simple as it is complex. You must practise the skill in the right way. Like any discipline, conscientious and enthusiastic practice will reward you."

"But how do I do that? How do I slow time down?"

"Just follow your star."

* * *

The Young Apprentice lay on his back in the sand. He could hear the stirring of the waves against the shore. He felt the warm breeze caress his body. The scent of the sea was in his nose, the tang of the salt on his tongue. He gazed up into the arched cobalt vault, and from the many thousands above him, he chose his one true star. He focused his gaze upon it, with conscientiousness and enthusiasm, and gradually it seemed to him, that the longer and deeper he gazed, all the other stars began to disappear from sight, until only his remained in the firmament. His own true star that he was destined to follow, for now, for ever …

Primary source: Wyatt Woodsmall.
Secondary influence: Konstantin Stanislavski.

1.14   *Lunchtime Learning*

The baby mouselets were only a few days old. And they were full of the joys of life. Under the watchful eye of their mother, they were jumping and tumbling, leaping and hopping, squeaking and squealing, and having a great time.

Suddenly they all froze in their tracks. A large black shadow had fallen across them and the space where they were playing.

Slowly they turned their little mouselet heads around to see the source of the shadow. There, standing crouched and ready to pounce, was a huge black tomcat. His yellow eyes were as big as plates, his whiskers were long and menacing, his teeth were yellow and sharp and dripping with saliva. If that cat could have said one word it would have been, "Lunchtime!"

Quick as a flash, the mother mouse leaped over the mouselings and occupied the space between them and the tomcat. Glaring into the tomcat's eyes, she barked loudly and with attitude: "Woof! Woof! Woof! Woof! Woof! Woof! Woof! Woof!"

The tomcat was so surprised it turned on its heels and shot off into the distance with its tail between its legs.

The mother mouse turned to the mouselings and said, "There you are my darlings, let that be a lesson to you. Never underestimate the importance of learning a second language."

Primary source: Hugh Lupton.

1.15 *Perceptual Positions*

Right and wrong are situational.

In the appropriate situation, nothing is wrong.

Without the appropriate situation, nothing is right.

What is right in one case is not what is right in another.

What is wrong in one case is not what is wrong in another.

Primary source: Nick Hindley.
General source: Taoist tradition.

1.16   St Augustine's Prayer

Lord
How is it we
Journey
To wonder at
The might of the mountains
The surge of the seas
The roaming of the rivers
The awesomeness of the oceans
And circling of the stars …

While we pass ourselves by
Without ever wondering?

Primary source: Joseph O'Connor & John Seymour, Introducing NLP.
See bibliography.
Secondary source: Attributed to St Augustine.

Section 2

Value Added

Value Added

"What are values?" asked the Young Apprentice.

"Values are the things that give us direction in our lives."

"How do you mean?"

"Well," said the Magician, "we tend to move towards what we value and away from what we don't. In other words, we pay attention to those things we think are important and disregard or delete information we don't think is important."

"Oh yes, I know what you mean. Last week I was at a seminar, and on day three the facilitator asked the delegates to close their eyes and say how many plants there were in the training room. There were many different answers, and some people even insisted there weren't any plants at all. In fact there were five, and it was interesting that the people who were most interested in plants were the ones who, generally speaking, got the right answer."

"Exactly so. Our values are filters. When we think about how rich the world is in information, it is amazing, isn't it, that our sensory apparatus is not overwhelmed by it all. If we noticed *everything* around us we wouldn't be able to operate effectively. So what happens? We pay attention almost exclusively to those things we value and ignore much of the rest."

"That must be why everyone has their own model of reality. We all live in the same world but we each experience it in unique and different ways. We pay attention to different things according to our personal value systems."

"Precisely," said the Magician. "The map is not the territory, even though people tend to behave as though it is. What's more, when we communicate our experience through language to ourselves and others, we delete even more information. We talk about the things that we most value or think others will value. We leave so much out that sometimes it's a wonder we understand each other at all."

"So why is this section of the book called Value Added?" asked the Little Apprentice.

"Well, the values we each hold predict the ways we behave towards ourselves and others, and the skills levels we choose to develop, or not, to enhance these behaviours."

"So I guess values must be pretty important. And I'm wondering now, are values fixed or can they change?"

"Some values are core values and may not change throughout your life. Other values, however, will change and as they change so your skills levels and behaviours may well change. Changes in certain key values may even change your sense of identity, how you perceive yourself, and how others perceive you."

"So are the stories in this section designed to get us thinking about the values we hold and their implications? Are these stories meant to challenge the values we currently hold to see whether they are appropriate or not? Are these stories meant to demonstrate that other people's value systems may be different but are equally as valid as our own, and that we can benefit by learning from them?"

"If you want to know all that, I guess you'll have to read them and decide for yourself," said the Magician.

2.01   Rules from the Book of the Earth

Think honestly and be true to yourself.

Practise to follow "The Way".

Be open to the learning of all arts.

Be curious about all professions.

Know the difference between gain and loss.

Pay attention to your conscious awareness.

Pay attention to those things that are beyond consciousness.

Pay attention to the smallest details.

Concern yourself only with what is useful.

Primary source: Christof Kunz.
Secondary source: The Book of the Earth, Miyamoto Musashi (Samurai tradition).

2.02   *Real Knowledge*

A Schoolmaster approached a certain well respected Teacher and accused her teachings of being illogical, psycho-babble, and numerous other unflattering things. The Teacher took from a hidden pocket a jewel. She pointed to the arcade in the shopping centre and said, "Take this jewel to the shops that sell silverware and watch batteries and see if you can get a hundred gold pounds for it."

The Schoolmaster tried many such stores but could get nothing more than the offer of a hundred silver sickles.

"Excellent," said the Teacher. "Now go to a real jeweller and see what he will give you."

The Schoolmaster went into the nearest jeweller's shop and was amazed to be offered, straightaway, ten thousand gold pounds for the jewel.

The Teacher said, "Your understanding of real knowledge, and of my teachings, is as the silverware sellers' understanding of jewellery. If you want to value precious stones, become a jeweller."

Primary source: Zulema Martinez.
Secondary source: Idries Shah, Thinkers of the East. See bibliography.
General source: Sufi tradition.

2.03   *The Priest*

The old priest came to the village only once every three months. It was a remote village tucked away deep among the mountain valleys. It was as far from the capital city as any village in the country. The people were simple, hardworking farmers. Their lives were governed by the stars and the seasons and, so the priest liked to believe, by his occasional visits.

The priest had known the community for many seasons; he had a strong fatherly interest in their affairs. Among all the people in the village he identified one particular boy as having something out of the ordinary, something indefinable and special. The boy seemed to have an intelligence and sensitivity that could not be easily discerned in his peers or elders. Like the priest, he seemed to be a boy marked out to lead.

When the boy was old enough, the priest arranged with the village elders to have the boy sent to the capital. The boy was to enter the seminary and study to become a priest, in order to return and lead his community in the way the old priest wished it.

And so the time came and the young man set out on his journey to the capital city. He began his journey on foot along precipitous paths tracking across steep mountains, and then by donkey, and then by cart, and then by train, so that after many days of travel he finally arrived at the gate of the seminary in the main square of the capital city.

And the boy studied hard, mindful of his debt of gratitude and obligation to the priest, and to his community who had saved hard to send him there. He loved the life, and the discipline, and the rituals, and the sense of community, learning, and devotion.

And so he worked diligently in every way that was required of him through the long years of apprenticeship, dedication, and service.

After several years a letter arrived. It was a letter from his village congratulating him on his imminent entry to the priesthood after so many years of study and discipline. The letter respectfully invited him to return to the village and share his experiences of all the things he had done and achieved in the capital city, a place where few villagers had ever been. The invitation asked him to share his experiences, in the village hall, with the whole community, and, as coincidence would have it, the invitation was for a day exactly one year on from the day he received the letter.

After the young seminarian had finished reading the letter he was filled with a troubling mixture of pride and humility. And he resolved to prepare a presentation for his village that would be all of many things: fitting his new status, yet humble and grateful for the sacrifices the community had made on his behalf; sharing the wonders of the capital city, yet mindful of the unsophisticated wisdoms of the countryside, and much more besides.

He became obsessed with the idea of preparing the perfect presentation. All his spare time he dedicated to working, honing, refining, his speech. Every evening after prayers he would wander around the cloister, the herb gardens, and the orchard, rehearsing parts of his masterpiece.

Finally, the day came that he was ordained, and soon after, he left the seminary. He took the train, then the cart, the donkey, and finally the precipitous trail that led him by foot to the village in the valley from where he had begun his journey so many years before.

He arrived at the appointed hour on the appointed day to deliver his presentation to his people in the village hall. But there was no one around. The village was deserted. He looked around, he knocked on doors, he shouted. There was nobody. He felt crestfallen. All that work, all that effort, all that energy, wasted. And the adrenaline that had been rushing through him in anticipation of performance began to drain out of his system.

At that moment, a stable boy appeared. Not remembering the young priest who had left the village so many years ago, the stable boy asked who he was. And the young priest told him, and told him of the invitation.

"Oh," said the stable boy, "they must have forgotten. They're all out at the farms. There's a huge harvest this year, which we have to get in before the rains. I'm the only one here. Someone's got to look after the horses."

The young priest asked the stable boy what he should do. "You see, I've been working on this speech for such a long time and it's as if it was bursting out of me, and now it seems to be all wasted. I've been working up to this moment for months and now ... Well, it's just so disappointing."

"Well," said the stable boy, "it's not really for me to tell you, Sir, seeing as how you're a fine educated priest and I'm just a stable boy. But, you know, if I came back to my stable after being away, and I found that all my horses had run away except one, of course I would feed that horse."

Hearing this, the young priest took heart. In gratitude he seized the young boy by the hand and together they entered the village hall. He sat the stable boy in the middle of the front row, and went up onto the stage. And he began his presentation.

And immediately it was as if he was filled with the spirit of his Creator. And he talked with eloquence and passion, with style and panache. His words were elegant and his sentences flowed, soaring with the tricks of ancient rhetoricians. He talked with pride and he talked with humility, he talked of his vision and he talked of his mission. He talked, and he talked, and he talked. Until finally he ran out of words. He glowed with the effort of his three-hour sermon, he was filled with enthusiasm, he was delighted to have had the opportunity to illuminate the life of this simple stable boy with words of wisdom.

And of course he wanted feedback, confirmation of his skill, and devotion.

"How was it?" he asked. "Did you like my presentation?"

"Well," said the stable boy, rubbing life back into his numb limbs, "as I said, Sir, it's not really my place to tell you what's what, being as I'm just a simple stable boy and you're a fine educated man. However, as I said before, if all my horses had run away except one, of course I would feed that horse ... But I wouldn't give it all the food I had."

Primary source: Tessa Woodward, Ways of Training, Longman.
Secondary source: Nossrat Peseschkian.
General source: Oriental tradition.

2.04   *The Quarryman*

The quarryman's work was hard. He worked all day in the quarry from dawn to dusk. His hands were hard and callused. His back was bent, and his face was weathered and lined.

He was not happy. He said, "This is no life. Why is it my fate to be a quarryman? Why can't I be someone who has more wealth than I do? If only I were rich, then I'd be happy."

An Angel appeared and said, "What would have to happen for you to know you were rich and happy?"

"That's easy. If I was rich I'd live in the city, in a beautiful apartment on the top floor. I'd be able to see the sky. I'd have a four-poster bed with cool black silk sheets, and I'd sleep all day. Then I'd be happy."

"You are rich," said the Angel waving her magic wand. And he became rich. And he lived in the city in an apartment on the top floor. And he slept all day in a four-poster bed with cool black silk sheets. And he was happy.

Until one day he was disturbed by a commotion in the streets below. He sprang out of bed and ran to the window. Looking down he saw a graceful golden carriage. In front were horses and behind were soldiers. It was the King. And the people who thronged the street were cheering and bowing.

The rich man instantly knew unhappiness. "I'm not happy. The king has more power than I do. If only I was the King, then I'd be happy."

And the Angel appeared and said, "You are the King!" And he became the King. And he was happy. He felt his power and he felt his might. And he loved the way people paid him homage, and the way his servants obeyed him, and the way he had power to decide whether others should live or die. He was happy.

And then one day he noticed Sun. And he saw how Sun had power to do things he couldn't even dream of. He saw how Sun could turn all the fields from green to yellow, and from yellow to brown. He saw how Sun could dry up even the mightiest rivers and leave nothing but parched mud banks. He saw how Sun could starve the world of life.

And he knew unhappiness. "I'm not happy. The Sun has more power than I do. If only I were the Sun, then I'd be happy."

And the Angel appeared and said, "You are the Sun!" And he became Sun. And he was happy. He felt his power and he felt his might. And he loved the way he could turn the fields from green to brown, dry up the rivers, and change the whole world. And he was happy.

And he ruled the world from his zenith, exulting in his power.

Until one day he noticed Cloud, big black Raincloud. And he saw how Cloud had the power to turn all the fields from brown to green, refill the rivers with flowing, frothing water, and retrieve the life of the world.

And depression filled him. "I'm so unhappy. This Cloud has more power than I. If only I was Cloud then I'd be happy forever."

And the Angel appeared and said, "You are Cloud." And he became Cloud, and he was happy. He felt his power and might. And he loved the way he could reverse the work of the Sun and re-instate life where so little had been before. And he knew real happiness for the first time.

Until one day he saw, far below him, Rock. And he saw how Rock, black, strong, unyielding, was unchangeable. And he saw that no matter how much or how hard he rained, nothing he could do could challenge or destroy Rock. Rock was rugged and resistant.

And he knew the bitterness of unhappiness once again. And he said, "I'm so unhappy. If only I were Rock then I'd be happy."

And the Angel appeared and said, "You are Rock." And he became Rock, and he felt his might and he felt his power, and he was happy. He exulted in his strength and sense of permanence. He loved his ability to withstand everything Nature could throw at him. He laughed at the Sun and he ridiculed Raincloud.

Until one day, a Quarryman arrived …

Primary source: John Morgan & Mario Rinvolucri, Once Upon A Time. See bibliography.
Secondary source: Scandinavian tradition.

2.05   True Holiness

A holy man was walking by the river considering the nature of true holiness. He was a precise man, who kept to the letter of the holy law, and considered it his holy duty to notice those frailties he detected in himself and others. He studied and prayed very hard so that he should become as perfect as possible.

As he walked by the river, reciting his prayers, he heard floating across the river from afar the holiest of the prayers of his order. The prayer, as was the custom, was repeated over and over again in order to induce a holy trance in the reciter.

But the prayer disturbed the holy man. Whoever was saying these prayers had failed to learn them correctly. The syllables of the first words of the prayer were in the wrong order. The holy man knew that a prerequisite for attaining bliss in the next life was an intention towards perfection in this life. And clearly the getting wrong of an important prayer was going to be a hindrance to the pilgrim across the river in his quest to achieve Paradise.

At this opportunity to do "good work" by correcting this misguided worshipper, the holy man rented a rowing boat and set out across the river to find the man who was mangling such holy and beautiful words.

As he was paddling across the lapping wavelets and negotiating the currents, his mind wandered to a curious phenomenon of holiness that he himself had never had the opportunity to witness. He considered that one would have to reach a very high level of holiness indeed to achieve the art of walking across water. Perhaps, if he was able to perfect himself a little more, and achieve greater saintliness through acts similar to the one that he was even now engaging in, to wit the important and necessary correction of a misguided sinner who hadn't taken sufficient trouble to learn his prayers properly, he himself might one day reach the level of sanctity sufficient to traverse the waves on foot.

And another thing. It was surely the duty of all right minded people to give advice and corrective feedback to those who erred.

Just as it was *their* duty to accept the advice and feedback with humility and without justification.

The mangled opening to the prayer broke through once again into his consciousness, disturbing his meditations on holiness and its higher manifestations. The sound was coming from an island in the river. He drew up to a small jetty, moored the boat, and walked up a short gravel path. Inside a small and simple cave he was much surprised to find another holy man of his order praying.

"Brother," said the perspiring rower, "I have taken the trouble to row all the way across this river to draw your attention to the fact that you are mis-saying your prayers. You are saying, 'Yee moo yen zaa' and you ought to be saying 'Yen moo zaa yee'."

"Thank you," said the hermit. "I feared that might be the case and am most grateful to you for the trouble to which you have put yourself. Would you care to repeat the correct form once again so that I might follow the more enlightened path?"

The holy man offered once again the correct version and then returned to his boat. As he paddled back across the river he reflected on the nature of good works and the duty of the moral man to restore true order to a misguided world. Acts of saintliness such as this were the signs and symbols that one was indeed on the true path to holiness and Paradise.

He was much surprised to be disturbed in his meditations on holiness by a voice calling to him.

"Wait a moment please, good sir," came the voice across the waves.

Looking up, the holy man saw the hermit walking rapidly across the waves towards him. "I'm terribly sorry to bother you again, but I'm afraid my memory is short and I am not the quickest of learners. Did you say it was 'Yen zaa moo yee' or 'Yen moo zaa yee'?"

"'Yen moo zaa yee'," echoed the holy man numbly.

"Thank you so much. May your good deed be richly rewarded."

And so saying, the hermit turned and walked lightly back across the water.

Primary source: Sandra Maitri.
Secondary source: Idries Shah.
General source: Sufi tradition.

2.06   *The Rewards of Study*

An ambitious young man had travelled far from his family and native land to study in a distant and foreign country. For seven years he applied himself with discipline and diligence to learn the art and science of physiognomy, the skill of detecting personality and character in the faces of others.

He qualified with honours and set off on the long journey back to his homeland. On his way he missed no opportunity to test his skills in reading the personality of others in their faces.

Travelling across a wide and inhospitable valley, where there was little provision or shelter available, the student met a man upon whose face was stamped the worst of all passions. In the leathery features of this man's face the student read greed, gluttony, lust, envy, anger, avarice, and foul intent.

But when the man approached the student, his face broke into a broad smile and with a warm, kind, and gentle voice he invited the student to stay with him and recover from the journey in his house. "It is but a simple place," the man told him, "but you are most welcome to rest from the rigours of your journey. Relax here and make yourself at home. What's mine is yours. Consider yourself my guest. Go no further tonight for the next village is far away."

The student was mightily confused by this. He feared that all his studies were wasted, that seven years of rigorous discipline was no more than the value of bottled air.

So in order to check his doubts and fears, the student accepted the invitation.

Such was the intensity of the man's desire to entertain his guest lavishly that the student found it extremely hard to leave. He was pampered with all kinds of sumptuous and tasty foods and delicacies. He was given the sweetest of aromatic nectars, and the most fragrant of teas and infusions to drink. Finally, after several days, the student determined to leave.

But when he prepared to mount his saddled horse, the man presented him with an envelope. "Here is your bill, sir."

The student was taken aback. "Bill? What are you talking about?"

The geniality of the host's face disappeared as swiftly as a rose in acid. He drew a wicked knife from his belt, and thrust it towards the student's face. His features returned to the malevolent aspect the student had first discerned. "Pay up, you cheating cheapskate. About to run off, were you? Thought you could get away without paying, eh? Do you think I'm made of money to provide you with all the best produce of this region for free? Typical scrounging student."

The student, who had been caught totally by surprise at this vicious attack and was mesmerised by the dagger held at his throat, suddenly snapped out of his inertia. He opened the envelope and read the bill in which he was charged for everything he had and hadn't eaten two hundred times over.

The money demanded was a staggering sum, far more than the student had with him. But with a broad smile wreathing his face and a lightness in his movement, the student dismounted from the horse and gave it to his former host. He removed his fine hat and travelling cape and handed these over too.

And with joy in every step, the student continued his journey, celebrating with his each and every breath the fact that his seven years of education had not been wasted after all.

Primary source: Nossrat Peseschkian.
Secondary source: Abdu'l-Baha.

2.07   Cape Canaveral

In the pioneering days of space research, John Kennedy was visiting NASA at the Cape. He had met many great scientists, and researchers. He had met the men whose great ambition was to conquer space and walk on the surface of the moon. He had met administrators and accountants, and many others whose contribution to the project was immense. Men and women who had a sense of destiny, purpose, and pride.

Walking through the corridors on his way back to his limousine, he came across a stooped, grey-haired black man with a bucket in one hand and a mop in the other. It seemed to be quite a redundant question, but the President asked him politely, "And what do you do here at the Cape?"

Straightening his back, the cleaner looked square at the President, and with a strong sense of pride and dignity in his voice replied: "Sir, I'm doing the same here as everybody else. I'm working here to put a man on the moon. That's exactly what I'm doing here."

Primary source: Judith DeLozier.

2.08   *Food for Thought*

It was mid-morning. Socrates had gone for a walk outside the city walls of Athens. He was taking a rest, sitting on a milepost on the road about five miles from the city.

Down by his right foot was a small parcel. And he was considering whether to open it now or leave it till later. In it was his lunch. It had been packed by his wife because in those days, that's what wives used to do … make lunch for their husbands.

His mind started to wander. He knew exactly what was inside that parcel. It was his favourite food. Greek salad. He began to imagine the contents in his mind's eye.

First there would be chunks of those luscious, juicy, bright red Mediterranean tomatoes. And he imagined how he would bite into them, taking care not to let all the juices explode over his shirt.

Then he thought about the piquant salty taste of the olives. He could feel them already rolling about in his mouth, round and smooth. Then he would spit the stones at passing mosquitoes.

He anticipated the sharp tang of those slices of pungent red onion and the cooling refreshing softness of the cucumber.

Above all he relished the thought of the creamy texture of the slices of sheep's cheese, salty and crumbling in his mouth, and all washed down with the very best extra virgin cold pressed olive oil of Attica. It was enough to make your mouth water just thinking about that!

He was tempted to have an early lunch, but just as he bent down to open the parcel a traveller came along the road and hailed him.

"Greetings, friend! Can you tell me, is this the right road for Athens?"

Socrates assured him that it was. "Carry straight on ahead. It's quite a big city. You can't miss it."

"Tell me," said the traveller, "what are the people of Athens like?"

"Well," said Socrates, "tell me where you come from, and what the people there are like, and I'll tell you about the people of Athens."

"I'm from Argos. And I'm proud and happy to tell you that the people of Argos are the friendliest, happiest, most generous people you could ever wish to meet."

"And I'm very happy to tell you, my friend," said Socrates, "that the people of Athens are exactly the same."

The traveller went on his way, and Socrates remained on his milestone. The conversation had made him feel like celebrating the goodness and humanity in the world. So his mind went to his wineskin, which was resting by his left foot. He wondered whether he should take a drink so early in the day. But the thought of that cool refreshing local wine, its heady mix of grape and pine kernel, was very tempting. He was imagining holding the wineskin at arm's length and squeezing a long refreshing arc of liquid ambrosia into his parched throat when another traveller came along the road.

"Greetings, friend! Can you tell me, is this the right road for Athens?"

As with the previous traveller, Socrates assured him that it was. "Carry straight on ahead. It's quite a big city. You can't miss it."

"Tell me," said the traveller, "what are the people of Athens like?"

"Well," said Socrates, "tell me where you come from, and what the people there are like, and I'll tell you about the people of Athens."

"I'm from Argos," said the second traveller, "and I'm sad and disappointed to tell you that the people of Argos are the meanest, most miserable, least friendly people you could ever wish to meet."

"And I'm very disappointed to tell you, my friend," said Socrates, "that the people of Athens are exactly the same."

Primary source: Mario Rinvolucri & Christine Frank, Challenge to Think, OUP.

2.09   *Tutta la Vita é Fuori*

In his book *Emotional Intelligence*, Daniel Goleman cites a case history concerning research into the visual processing of information in monkeys.[1] In the research, a young monkey with perfect eyesight had had one eye bandaged over during the critical period of visual development, around eight months in all. It emerged in the research findings that, although the bandaged eye could actually see, it could not make the fine distinctions and discriminations of which the other eye was capable.

The previously bandaged eye could not distinguish speed, distance, colours, relationship, and so on with anything like the skill of the unbandaged eye. Those parts of the brain which control visual development clearly needed rich and constant stimulation to reach their full potential.

No doubt this is as true for the development of the other senses as it is for the visual system. And yet in some households and in many schools around the world there is a marked absence of rich and varied sensory stimulation. And the child's brain takes a much longer time to achieve full development than that of a monkey, taking years rather than months.

There is a school in Ancona, on the east coast of Italy, where I ran a teacher development programme some years ago. We parked the car in the school playground, and as we entered the school through large glass double doors I was in animated conversation with some colleagues about the structure of how we would run the course. I didn't notice much until I was inside the building.

The drabness of colours had an instant depressing effect on me. Above a one-metre mark the walls were dull military khaki, below the line a faded beige. There was not a single work of art on any wall in any of the public spaces, hall or corridors, neither by Italian masters nor by the students themselves. The lighting was dim and cold. The school possessed all the excitement of a morgue.

Inside the classrooms, things were no better. Apart from timetables there was a marked absence of any visual stimulation on the walls. They were bare.

It was one of the most depressing environments in which I have ever worked. It took enormous amounts of energy to generate in myself an enthusiasm and commitment necessary to engage with the group. And I sensed their sense of gloom too.

It was only when I left the building in the early evening, leaving through the same double glass doors through which I had entered some hours earlier, that I noticed the reaction the inner environment had elicited from the students. On each side of the doors the students had set about the formless concrete with their spray cans. They had created some beautiful graffiti on both sides of the entrance, colourful, imaginative, and expressive.

And right in the centre of the left-hand graffiti were the words in Italian: *Tutta la Vita é Fuori.* All life is on the outside.

---

[1] Daniel Goleman, *Emotional Intelligence*. London: Bloomsbury, 1996.

2.10   Perception

I had been in the Italian seaside town for almost a week. Working all day and free to do as I pleased in the evening. Unfortunately, it was February. Fortunately, this gave me time to indulge a passion of mine, Italian food. Unfortunately, it was hard to locate good restaurants out of season. Fortunately, on the last day somebody mentioned the Z Bass restaurant.

Standing outside the glass door, I knew it was going to be a good choice. It was full. Only one table was vacant. Opening the door was like stepping into a world of pleasure and sensation. First was the rich smell of fish stew, *zuppe di pesce,* the house speciality. Then the vibrant chatter of Italians enjoying themselves. And, of course, the waiters with brightly striped waistcoats holding aloft steaming platters, smiling, shouting to each other and behaving as if they were born to wait in a way that seems unique to Italian waiters.

I sat down at my table and ordered. Across from my small table, a much larger table was occupied by twelve men, six each side. Perhaps they were relatives, or workmates. At any rate they were celebrating something and were well into their meal of *zuppe di pesce*.

The man sitting opposite me, against the wall, caught my attention. He was ugly. His face was deformed, stretched and misshapen, ravaged by some disease. He seemed like an elephant man, and certainly the ugliest man I had ever seen. I knew I shouldn't look, but in the way that a tongue seeks incessantly a missing tooth, my eyes kept wandering back.

I began to notice what he was doing. He was eating *zuppe di pesce*. He would bring the spoon slowly up to his mouth, his whole face expectant with anticipation. His eyes would shine and then close and he would hold the stew in his mouth, letting it melt and cool slowly. Each spoonful took minutes to savour. He extracted every last taste from each mouthful as if tasting some food reserved only for gods.

He would take three spoonfuls in this way and then put his spoon down. Then he reached over and took a cigarette from the packet in front of him. He lit it in the same deliberate way that he ate the food and then inhaled each pull deep into the centre of his being. A smile suffused his face, and a frisson passed through his body. He made cigarette smoking seem an art form, an act more desirable than any other sensual pleasure. It was as if each pull would be the last before the firing squad ended his life, and he wished to extract as much as humanly possible from each last moment.

I began to realise how wrong I had been in my former assessment. This man was not ugly. He was able to do something that is very special, something that I have long desired to do better myself.

This man knew how to live in the present moment, to extract as much experience as possible from the *now*. While some people look back to the past for reference, many others worry about what is to come, thinking how to plan and organise their future. These things are of course important. But it takes a special kind of wisdom to appreciate that each present moment is precious, full of experience, and will never come again. Far from being ugly, perhaps this was the most beautiful man I had ever seen. And to this day I thank him for his *present*.

2.11 *Motivation*

Most people, in any European state, if they are asked whether there are outside toilets where they live, say, "No! We're a developed country."

But if asked, "And do they have wooden doors with a small heart or diamond cut out near the top?" they nod and say, "Oh yes, my grandmother has one exactly like that."

And you know how it is with outside toilets. They still exist for a variety of reasons, such as the following.

Nostalgia: my Granny used to sit and meditate on the meaning of life in there.

Practicality: it's not worth knocking it down, it's too useful for storing all the gardening tools.

Inertia: it's just too much trouble to demolish it.

And above all, self-interest: when someone's using the indoor one and you're desperate, well, it's just ideal.

Of course, outside ones don't get cleaned as often as indoor ones do. And these days they are very old. They've been there a long time. And so over the years sediment and all kinds of other stuff has accumulated down there at the bottom.

And it's exactly in this kind of outside toilet that our story takes place.

Imagine the scene if you will, a man standing, about to do what a man sometimes has to do. And he's gazing down into the murky mysterious waters. When suddenly he notices something bright down there, shining up at him. It's glittering, sparkling, and brilliant. It's a mint-fresh British two-pound coin.

His reaction is immediate and human. A voice in his head says, "That could be mine," and he begins to roll up his shirtsleeve. But suddenly he stops.

And the voice says, "But is it worth it?"

And he considers a moment or two, contemplating what to do. And then he has a brilliant idea.

He puts his hand in his pocket. Takes out another bright, shiny, sparkling two-pound coin. Looks at it for a moment or two. And then throws it down into the murky depths so it's resting next to the other one.

Then he rolls up his sleeve with purpose.

And he says, "Now it's worth it!"

Primary source: David Gordon.

2.12   Learning the Rules

In his book *Steps to an Ecology of Mind*, Gregory Bateson describes certain aspects of his work studying communication patterns among dolphins. He tells of his time at the Marine Research Centre in Hawaii where he was observing the training of dolphins.

On the first day, when the dolphin did something unusual, the trainer blew her whistle and threw the dolphin a fish. Every time the dolphin repeated exactly the same behaviour, for example a leap, it would earn another fish. The dolphin soon learned that to repeat this behaviour guaranteed it a reward.

On the next day, the dolphin would repeat the trick. No fish. The dolphin would repeat it several times without reward until in frustration it would do something else, like a barrel roll. The trainer then blew her whistle and threw the dolphin a fish. The dolphin quickly learned that when it repeated this new trick it could expect a reward. No fish for yesterday's trick; only fish for a new trick.

This pattern continued for a fortnight. Every day the dolphin would repeat yesterday's trick without reward, become frustrated, and do something else. If the behaviour was a new one, the trainer blew her whistle, and threw the dolphin a fish. By the end of the fourteenth day, the dolphin had developed and practised a repertoire of 14 tricks.

On the fifteenth day, the dolphin appeared to have learned the rules of the game. It had made some connections and moved up a learning level. Instead of accidentally discovering a fish-getting activity through frustration, it actively discovered how the mechanisms worked and how to achieve the rewards it wanted.

On the morning of the fifteenth day the dolphin swam into the training pool and performed a tour de force. As well as executing many of the tricks it had learned in the previous days, it performed eight completely new behaviours, four of which had never been observed in the species before.

The dolphin, it appeared, had learned not only how to generate new behaviours, but the rules governing where, when, and how to generate them.

Bateson mentions one other powerful insight into the mechanisms of learning. Outside of the training environment during the first fortnight of training, Bateson would sometimes see the trainer throwing the dolphin an unearned fish. When Bateson inquired why this was so, the trainer replied, "To keep my relationship with him. If I don't build a relationship with the dolphin, he's not going to bother to learn anything."

Primary source: Ian McDermott.
Secondary source: Gregory Bateson.

2.13   The Perfectionist

A perfectionist came across an injured hawk huddling for safety in a doorway. He picked it up and examined it.

"Oh dear, you poor thing," he exclaimed. "What sort of a bird are you? You're not quite right."

He took out a pair of scissors and removed the ugly curve in its upper beak so it sat neat and even on top of the lower one. Then he clipped and trimmed its swept-back wings so they were straight. Finally he took his nail clippers to the hawk's talons and cut them right back to the toes.

"There," he said, admiring his handiwork. "Now you look much more like a bird ought to look."

Primary source: Sandra Maitri.
General source: Sufi tradition.

2.14   *The Value of Time*

A businessman had amassed a fortune that amounted to three million pounds of gold dollars. He decided that he would take a year off from work and live in the kind of luxury that his wealth allowed him.

But no sooner had he made this decision than the Angel of Death beckoned him.

The man, who was a skilful negotiator, tried every argument he could think of to dissuade the Angel and to buy himself more time. But the Angel of Death was adamant; the man's time had come.

In final desperation, the rich man made the Angel an offer. "Give me three more days of life and I will give you a third of my wealth, a million pounds of gold dollars."

The Angel refused.

"Give me two more days of life and I will give you two thirds of my wealth, two million pounds of gold dollars."

The Angel again refused.

"Give me one more day of life, to enjoy this beautiful and bountiful planet, and to spend a little time with my family who I have neglected for too long, and I will give you all of my wealth. Three million pounds of gold dollars."

But the Angel could not be persuaded.

Finally, the man asked if the Angel would just grant him a little time to write a short paragraph. And this wish was granted.

Make good use of your time on earth, he wrote. I could not buy even one hour of life for three million pounds of golden dollars. Be sure to know in your heart what things in your life are of true value, and place your attention there.

Primary source: Idries Shah, The Way of the Sufi. See bibliography.
General source: Sufi tradition.

2.15   The Caged Bird

The bird in the cage had lived there for a very long time. Often it would look through the bars of the cage, out of the window to the meadows and trees beyond. It could see other birds flying free in the open air and often it would wonder how it would be to feel the sun on its back, the wind in its feathers, to swoop and soar and snatch mosquitoes in flight.

When the bird thought of these things it could feel its heart beating with excitement. It would sit taller on its perch and breathe deep into its bird belly, sensing the thrill of possibility.

Sometimes another bird would land on the window sill, resting from its travels, and look inside at the caged bird. The traveller would put its head on one side as if quizzically asking itself how such a thing could be. A bird in a cage. Unimaginable.

And it was at these times that the caged bird felt most miserable. Its little shoulders slumped, it felt a lump in its throat and a heaviness in its heart.

One day, the owner of the caged bird accidentally left the door of the cage open. The bird looked through the door. It saw the birds swooping and soaring outside, the sun on their backs and the wind in their feathers, and it felt a stirring inside. The caged bird noticed that the window was open, and its heart beat even faster.

It considered its options.

It was still considering them at sunset when the owner returned and closed the door of the cage.

The bird, for whatever reasons, valued security over freedom.

Primary source: David Werner & Bill Bower, Helping Health Workers Learn, Hesperian Foundation.

Section 3

Structures and Patterns

Structures and Patterns

"Why structures and patterns?" asked the Young Apprentice.

"Your brain is a meaning-making organisation," replied the Magician. "It actively seeks out patterns in order to impose meaning and understanding on events and information. It seeks out relationships between things and organises the results into hierarchies of information that will be easy to store and remember. It chunks up to generalisation and abstraction and chunks down to detail and precision."

"Can you give me an example?"

"Sure, here's a simple one. How do you remember the colours of the rainbow in the correct sequence?"

"That's easy: VIBGYOR!"

"Exactly, your mnemonic VIBGYOR is a generalisation, a higher level of information than the details it triggers: violet, indigo, blue, green, yellow, orange, red."

"I see."

"Although life can seem chaotic, random, and unstructured, it is useful to understand that everything has a structure, although it is usually concealed below the surface of things or in your unconscious knowledge. Every behaviour, every skill, every belief you have or hold has a structure, a pattern that supports it and holds it in place. The more you are aware of this structure, and how effective or ineffective the pattern is, the more control you will have over your life. You will be able to improve an effective pattern if you wish, or change entirely an ineffective one."

"How do you do that?" asked the Apprentice with a certain degree of scepticism.

"OK. How do you catch those fat trout on those days we have barbecues?"

"Oh! How do I tickle them? Well, you know, I have certain strategies for that."

"Exactly," said the Magician. "Strategies are the patterns in people's thought processes. There are effective strategies and ineffective strategies. Effective strategies will always succeed in getting you the results you want. Ineffective strategies will always succeed in getting you the results you don't want or don't expect. Either way, strategies are always successful in getting some result or other. So how do you tickle trout?"

"Well," said the Young One, his eyes bright with the memory. "First I place my hand in the water where the trout run, and I wait patiently till one swims my way. Then very carefully, when it gets near, I move my hand underneath its belly and begin to stroke it very gently. I check my stroking is in time with the rhythm of the movement of its gills; I wait until I feel a specific change in the muscle tone of its body against my finger; and then when I notice its eyes begin to lose focus and glaze over, I strike!"

"And if you strike without those conditions being met?" "Then I lose the fish," replied the Apprentice.

"So noticing that each one of those conditions has been met is your test for knowing that your strategy for catching trout will be successful."

"Yes, exactly."

"So now you know your strategy, your thinking pattern for catching fish."

"Gosh. I never realised exactly how I did all that before."

"So when we begin to understand the patterns that lie below our conscious awareness of things we not only begin to realise just how skilful and brilliantly organised our mind-body system can be, we can also begin to teach our skills to other people."

"And is this what I'll read about in this section of the book?"

"And much else besides."

3.01   *Designer Genes*

Everything has a structure. When you drive a car you follow a certain pattern of behaviours in a particular sequence if you wish to accelerate smoothly and safely away from the traffic lights. The same is true for all behaviours and all skills. Following the same patterns in the same sequence, all other things being equal, will always give you the same results.

The ability to seek and identify structures, patterns, and designs below the apparent surface of experience is the secret to success in communication, relationships, accelerated learning, languages, and many other things besides.

This is not a new idea. The Magician recalled a story from an ancient tradition.

A tinsmith was falsely accused and imprisoned. Being poor, he had no powerful friends to influence the judge. He passed each day considering the various choices that were open to him, for he had no desire to waste his life in jail, especially for something he hadn't done. But the jail was secure, and the warders were vigilant.

One day his wife brought him a prayer mat, and every day, five times a day, he prayed on it.

After a while he made a suggestion to his guards. "I am poor, and it seems probable that I'll end my days in prison. You are poor too, and poorly paid. What can we do?

"I am a tinsmith by trade. I have a skill but lack what I need. If you bring me tools and materials I can fashion metal into things that you can sell in the market. You will gain and so will I."

The guards agreed. They brought the things the tinsmith requested, and soon they were making profits. The tinsmith bought good food to supplement his meagre rations, and the guards bought the things they'd always wanted.

Then one morning the guards woke up to find the jail door open and the tinsmith gone. Some spoke of magic or perhaps a miracle because no prison in the eastern kingdom was considered more secure.

Many years later a convicted thief confessed to a crime he had committed long ago. As a result, the innocence of the tinsmith was established and he was pardoned in his absence. Two weeks later the tinsmith and his family reappeared.

The governor of the province, curious to know what had happened so many years before, summoned the tinsmith to his palace.

When asked how he had opened the prison door and escaped, the tinsmith said, "It is a question of patterns, and patterns within patterns. Or call it design if you wish.

"My wife is a weaver. She designs rugs, mats, and carpets. She weaves patterns into the wefts and warps of her fabric.

"By design she found the man who made the lock of the cell door and got it from him, by design.

"She wove the design of the lock into the fabric of the prayer mat she made for me. And as I prayed my head touched that very place where by design she had woven the key to the lock. As a tinsmith I recognised the pattern as the design of the inside of a lock.

"But I lacked materials and tools. By design I suggested a business proposition to my guards. I then designed certain things that could be sold in the market, ensuring the materials I needed for these artefacts would be what I needed to make the key.

"And so, by design, I escaped."

"We are all born with a brain," the Magician said, "but with no instructions about how to use it. The brain is an instrument of the most amazing power. But many people never learn how to use it effectively. This is a pity because effective ways of thinking and using our brain can be taught and learned.

"When we begin to understand the patterns and structures of our thinking, we can start to liberate ourselves from enslavement to our limitations."

Primary source: Sandra Maitri (Tinsmith story).
Secondary source: Idries Shah (Tinsmith story) acknowledging an unnamed Sufi from the Naqshbandi Order. "Naqshbandi" literally means "the designers".

3.02   *The Secret of Success*

And so the little boy went to his father and said, "Dad! Dad! What's the secret of success in life?"

His father said, "Son, that's a very difficult question. And I'm not the one to give you an answer. Why don't you ask your mother?"

So the little boy went to his mother and said, "Mum! Mum! What's the secret of success in life?"

His mother said, "Son, that's a very difficult question. And I'm not the one to give you an answer. Why don't you wait till the summer holidays and go see the Wise One who lives in the castle. The Wise One is sure to know."

And so with barely concealed excitement and anticipation the little boy waited through the winds of autumn, the frosts of winter, the unfurling of spring, and the promise of early summer until the holidays arrived.

He packed his rucksack with all the things he might need and set off for the distant castle of the Wise One. He walked the lengths of deep valleys, climbed across high mountains, crossed fast rivers, swam broad lakes, and trekked through dense forests until finally he reached the castle.

In the courtyard he was amazed to find it packed with people of every description. All were waiting to receive learning and knowledge from the Wise One. He was surprised that so many people from so many walks of life could be so interested in learning wisdom. There were actors, dancers, and painters. There were lawyers, doctors, and teachers. There were butchers, bakers, and candlestick makers. There were businesspeople, bankers, and accountants. There were housewives and househusbands. There were bus drivers, plumbers, and electricians. There were doctors, nurses, and people from the social services. There were even some politicians and academics.

The little boy waited patiently in turn. Finally he arrived before the Wise One. "Please tell me," he asked, "what is the secret of success in life?"

"Son," said the Wise One, "that's a very difficult question. And while I'm thinking of an answer, take time to visit my castle and appreciate all its wonder and beauty.

"Remove your shoes, for it is the custom in this land, and feel the smooth coolness of the mosaic floors in my reception rooms.

"Take a look at the fine hanging tapestries in my bedrooms, noticing the richness of their colours and the detail of their description.

"Take time to listen to the harmonious music of my musicians for the sounds they make will delight and enchant your ears and your soul.

"Be sure to visit my kitchens and taste the foods that my chefs produce, for the food they make, whether piquant or sweet, salt or sharp, sour or hot, spicy or subtle, will excite your senses as never before.

"And do not miss my gardens and orchards. For the sweet smells of the fruit in blossom and the tart aromas of the herbs will transport you to a land of long forgotten memories."

As the little boy was about to leave, the Wise One stopped him, and took out from a concealed cloak pocket a small spoon and a bottle.

"Just one thing before you go. Take this spoon and be sure," the Wise One said, putting two drops of oil from the bottle onto the spoon, "that under no circumstances you spill these two precious drops.

"Be back in two hours and I will answer your question."

* * *

Exactly two hours later the little boy returned. The Wise One asked, "And did you feel the cool texture of my floors, see the deep richness of my tapestries, inhale the powerful aromas from my gardens, taste the delicious fare prepared by my chefs, and hear the sweet sounds of my musicians?"

The little boy shook his head and said, "No. No. I did none of these things. But look, I still have the two drops of oil on my spoon."

The Wise One paused for a moment. And then said, "My son, never trust anyone whose house you do not know. Go back again. This time take all the time you need to appreciate all there is to be appreciated. This time use the powers of all your senses to notice the richness and glory that is around you. And then return once again, having noticed everything that is remarkable, with the spoon and the two drops of oil."

And so the little boy revisited the castle. When he returned four hours later he was ecstatic. His whole body was lithe and fluid, his eyes shone, his gestures were broad and expansive.

Full of wonder and amazement, he spoke to the Wise One. "Oh it's wonderful, all so wonderful. I saw the tapestries with their deep colours and fine details. I heard the rich and mellow strains of the musicians. I tried each and every one of the mouth-watering tastes in the kitchens. I smelled each of all the perfumes in the gardens and orchards; and I felt the cool smoothness of the mosaics on the soles of my feet. Everything here is completely wonderful."

"Yes indeed it is," said the Wise One. "It is completely wonderful. But what has become, may I ask, of the drops of oil that were on your spoon?"

And, of course, in his excitement the little boy had dropped the precious oil.

"The secret of success in life," said the Wise One, "is really very simple. In order to absorb, understand, and use the richness of the world that surrounds you, pay attention through every one of your five senses, for each is a priceless gift. Only then will you begin to notice how the whole world conspires to serve you in reaching whatever it is you want.

"And as you begin to discover how to move in the direction you desire, engaging with all the resources that surround you, you must equally learn to place your attention with care and flexibility. So just as you notice how magnificent and wonderful the whole world is, you must equally never cease to pay attention to the drops of oil on your spoon."

Primary source: Paolo Coelho, The Alchemist. See bibliography.

3.03   *Knowing Where to Tap*

At the end of the nineteenth century, a mill owner in the north of England was beside himself with worry. The steam boiler that provided light and power throughout his entire factory had broken down. Many experts had been to repair it but none had been successful. "Time is money," he kept repeating to himself as he counted the costs of lost production. "Time is money."

At this point a man in blue overalls was shown into his office. "I can repair your system, Sir," he said.

The mill owner was unimpressed. "I've had the best there are here to repair the boiler and they've all failed. Look at you, you've only got one small tool bag and not too much in it, if I'm not mistaken."

"Correct, sir. For this job I'll just need the tools necessary for this particular problem. Now, are you willing to let me fix it?"

Still unimpressed, but thinking he had nothing to lose, the mill owner led the man in blue overalls to the boiler room. In the centre of the room stood the boiler. Issuing from it were miles and miles of piping snaking towards every corner of the factory. From the boiler and pipes sounds of knocking, clunking, and hissing could be heard. But it was the absence of the din of machinery in operation that was most deafening.

In a somewhat patronising tone the owner invited the man to get on with it. Quietly and without fuss, the man in the blue overall selected one tool from his tool kit, a small rubber mallet.

Silently and methodically, he began to tap gently in various places, listening carefully to the responses he got from the metalwork. For ten minutes he tapped at pressure valves, at thermostats, at U-bends, at collars and joints where he diagnosed problems might exist. Finally, he returned to his tool bag, replaced his small mallet and selected a much larger one.

He stepped up to a complex elbow at one section of piping and gave it a firm and powerful thump with the mallet. The effect was instantaneous. As if a log jam had been shifted, water began to flow, steam began to pump, machines began to chatter.

The owner was delighted. "Marvellous, marvellous. Send me the bill. Double your normal price."

"That won't be necessary, sir," said the man in blue overalls.

When the bill arrived some days later, the owner was stunned. The amount was far more than he had expected. One hundred pounds sterling in all. A huge sum for those days. Although he had paid as much to some of the other companies who had failed to fix the system, they had been there for days. And they were companies with a reputation! The man in the blue overalls had been there for only ten minutes.

The mill owner instructed his secretary to send a reply asking for a breakdown of the costs.

The reply came by return of post.

For ten minutes of tapping	£1.00
For knowing where to tap	£99.00
	£100.00

Primary source: Julian Russell.
Secondary sources: There are many versions of this story, for example, Peseschkian.

3.04   The Littlest God

It wasn't long after the Gods had created humankind that they began to realise their mistake. The creatures they had created were so adept, so skilful, so full of curiosity and the spirit of inquiry that it was only a matter of time before they would start to challenge the Gods themselves for supremacy.

To ensure their pre-eminence the Gods held a large conference to discuss the issue. Gods were summoned from all over the known and unknown worlds. The debates were long, detailed, and soul-searching.

All the Gods were very clear about one thing. The difference between them and mortals was the difference between the quality of the resources they had. While humans had their egos and were concerned with the external, material aspects of the world, the Gods had spirit, soul, and an understanding of the workings of the inner self.

The danger was that sooner or later the humans would want some of that too.

The Gods decided to hide their precious resources. The question was: where? This was the reason for the length and passion of the debates at the Great Conference of the Gods.

Some suggested hiding these resources at the top of the highest mountain. But it was realised that sooner or later the humans would scale such a mountain.

And the deepest crater in the deepest ocean would be discovered.

And mines would be sunk into the earth.

And the most impenetrable jungles would give up their secrets.

And mechanical birds would explore the sky and space.

And the moon and the planets would become tourist destinations.

And even the wisest and most creative of the Gods fell silent as if every avenue had been explored and found wanting.

Until the Littlest God, who had been silent until now, spoke up.

"Why don't we hide these resources inside each human? They'll never think to look for them there."

Primary source: Peter McNab.

3.05   *Thinking Differently*

Eddie was a boy who had failed throughout his school years. He appeared a threat to his teachers. He would not conform. He seemed to have potential, but in his teachers' eyes he seemed to go out of his way to be "difficult". He was a born mismatcher. A misfit in the miseducation system.

He left school at 15 without grades or qualifications. He applied for a job in a government-run warehouse. And it being a government-run warehouse, there had to be a government-approved interview, conducted by a government-approved interviewer. And the interviewer, like the teachers, expected the right answer to the government-approved questions.

"OK," said the interviewer, "first, a general knowledge question. How many days of the week begin with the letter T?" Even the interviewer was surprised by the time it took Eddie to answer. Finally Eddie said, "Two."

"Correct," said the interviewer, "By the way, what are they?"

"Today and tomorrow," Eddie replied.

"OK," said the interviewer, thinking, 'I'll fix you, wise guy' under his breath. "Here's a mathematics question. How many seconds are there in a year?"

Quick as a flash Eddie replied, "Twelve."

"Twelve," echoed the interviewer with incredulity. "How the heck did you get that answer?"

"Well, that's easy," said Eddie. "There's January second, February second, March second, April ……………"

"OK. OK. Here's a spelling question. How many Ds are there in Rudolph the Red Nosed Reindeer?"

Again there was a long silence. Eddie seemed engaged in some complicated internal computation, nodding his head rhythmically. Finally, he said, "A hundred and three."

"A hundred and three? A hundred and three? Where do you get that answer from?"

"Da da da da da da dah. Dah da da da dah dah dah. Dah da ...."

Primary source: Michael Grinder, Righting the Educational Conveyor Belt. See bibliography.

3.06   Two Little Boys

Several summers ago a teacher was sitting on a sea wall resting after a long hike on the Cornish Coastal Path. She was eating a sandwich and observing events on the beach. Two young boys, around six years old, were playing together. They'd been running around for a while, having fun, and now, a little tired from their activities, they sat down near her and began talking.

Perhaps they'd just met, as children easily do on holiday; at any rate they seemed to have a lot to talk about. Finally, one said to the other, "What do you want to be when you grow up? I'm going to be a brain surgeon."

"Gosh. I don't really know. I've never thought about it. I'm not very bright, you know."

The Cornish wind took the rest of their conversation away. And the teacher was left wondering where that second little boy developed his limiting belief about himself. Probably from another teacher! Or a parent. At the age of six, if he doesn't change that belief, or if someone else doesn't help him to change it, it will affect the rest of his life, limiting his sense of possibility, holding back his potential.

Beliefs are not true. They are constructs around which we organise our behaviours. So we each behave as if our beliefs were true. And for this reason all our beliefs come true, for beliefs, whether empowering or limiting, are self-fulfilling prophecies.

Primary source: Sue Knight, NLP at Work. See bibliography.

3.07   *Talking the Same Language*

An Egyptian Professor of Business Studies at the University of Cairo attended a course on learning styles to find out how people learn in different ways. She discovered many new things. She learned, for example, that we all live in the same world, the same reality, but that we each understand and experience it differently.

"How do people learn?" asked the tutor. The group looked blank. "OK. Try it this way. How does information from the outside world enter your mind and your body?"

"That's easy," said one of the group. "Through our five senses."

"Precisely, there's no other way in. Our experience of the world is sensory-based. And because our experience is based on the senses, it is hardly surprising that our language has a sensory basis too, if you *see* what I mean? Can you *grasp* that? Does it *sound* OK? Take time to *savour* this point, *chew* it over, *digest* it, and then *tell* me whether it *makes sense*."

The group began to appreciate the point.

"However, we don't all use our senses in the same way. Each one of you can use all the senses that are available to you, and you can take in information through each of these sensory channels, but each of you will have preferences as to how you take in information best."

"Can you give me an example?" asked one of the group.

"Let me give you a rather extreme example," said the tutor, "by way of illustration. Four brothers go together to a club. On the way home in the early hours of the morning, they meet up with a friend.

"'How was the evening?'" asks the friend.

"The first brother replies, 'It was brilliant. The lighting was fantastic, there was an imaginative choice of music, and I saw a lot of mates. Great scene!'

"The second brother replies, 'It was spellbinding. Dynamic sounds. Great resonance. Spoke to a lot of mates. Yeah, it really gave me a buzz.'

"The third brother replies, 'Knock-out! The music really grabbed me. I got a real kick out of it. Made contact with loads of mates. Riveting.'

"The fourth brother replies, 'It was sweet. The music was really tasty, though one song brought back some bitter memories. Toasted my mates. Sharp!'"

"I think I see what you're saying," said one of the delegates excitedly. "The first one notices information through his eyes, the second through his ears, the third through his sense of touch and movement, and the fourth through his sense of taste."

"Precisely," said the tutor, "although this is a rather artificial illustration. Each of us has all our senses available to us. But most of us prefer to take in information and process it through one or two of our senses rather than use them all equally. If you listen to people's language, the sensory language patterns that are predominant may often give you a clue as to how a person is thinking. In other words, is the person thinking in pictures, in words or sounds, tactilely or emotionally?"

"So would I be right in supposing," offered one of the delegates, "that if somebody is talking to me and I detect a lot of visual based words like *see, imagine, reflect, mirror, look, unclear, dim, sparkling*, and so on then it would be an effective way to build a relationship if I matched him with visual language?"

"Precisely. And if you offered him back mainly auditory or kinaesthetic language instead, he might simply *see* you as being *distant, unfocused*, and only *dimly* aware of his *point of view*."

At this point a light bulb switched on for the Egyptian professor. "I think I've just seen the light," she said. "I can see how useful all of this will be for communicating in different ways with my students. I'll need to use powerful language, vary my vocal range, and include more question-and-answer sessions for my auditory preference learners. I'll need to have good quality and varied visual information to illustrate what I'm saying for my visual preference learners. And for those who prefer to learn kinaesthetically—through activity, hands-on learning, and emotional engagement—I'll need to include more task-based activities, group work, projects, presentations, and so forth.

"But what I can see most clearly," her tone was getting brighter now, "is that I have a new perspective to share with my family."

"What do you mean?" asked a neighbour.

"Well, what I've understood from this seminar is that, in most contexts, I have a strong visual preference. It's important to me how I appear to others; I take pride in how I look. And I see to it that our apartment is always neat, tidy, and organised. Everything has its place." She paused for a moment. "However, my husband and son, much as I love them, are rather different. Sometimes they make me see red. And now I begin to understand more about what that difference is."

"Go on," urged the neighbour, curious now.

"Well, my husband is very good really. He does make an effort to do the right things. He eats lunch at home by himself because the university, where I work, is too far away for me to get back to at midday. And he does do his best. He washes everything afterwards and puts it all away. The problem is that he puts most things back in the wrong places so I have to re-arrange it all when I get home—I love things to be in their proper places—and he has no idea how to wash glassware properly, so I have to clean a lot of the things all over again.

"And as for my son, he's sixteen and I love him dearly, but his room looks like a refugee camp. Clothes all over the floor, schoolbooks scattered around, piles of dirty washing, how he finds anything I have no idea.

"Well, to cut a long story short, I often let them know what I think about all this, and I have—regrettably—acquired the reputation of being something of a nag. But now I have some ideas, and I'll tell you what I'll do. After I've put my new insights into action and seen how they work, I'll let you know what happens. I'll write you all an e-mail so you can all see for yourselves how I got on."

A month or so later the tutor and the delegates on the seminar each received the following e-message:

My dear fellow seminarians,

When I got home after so much time away, I was greeted by my husband and son on the doorstep. We hugged and kissed, and it was wonderful to see them. As I went inside I happened to mention that there was something I wanted to talk to them about. My husband replied that if it had anything to do with the state of the apartment I should forget it. And of course it was. I could see over my husband's shoulder that it would need some serious cleaning and re-organising.

So I replied that if they just sat down on the sofa and gave me three minutes of their time I would never say another word about it. "What never," they said incredulously; "You'll never nag us again about the mess?"

"Sure," I said.

So they sat down and waited, curious to know what I had to say.

*"Imagine how it would be …" I began. And then checked myself. "No, how would it **feel** if you were lying in bed on a weekend morning. You are relaxed and comfortable, and at peace with yourself and the world." I saw a moment of recognition in their faces and watched as they began to relax and sit back into the sofa, connecting with the idea.*

"You have nothing to do all day except take your time to be at one with yourself. You can feel the sensation of your skin against the cool, clean, fresh cotton sheet. And while you are doing that you can feel your muscles beginning to relax and your spine stretching out, and you are feeling very, very contented."

They said nothing, but they looked as if they were in Paradise.

"You can smell the aroma of freshly brewed coffee, which our neighbours are preparing downstairs, carried through the window on the cool

morning breeze." At this point my husband's nose twitched and my son licked his lips.

"I bring you breakfast in bed, your favourite food, and you take time to savour every last mouthful, enjoying each and every taste, smell, and texture. And while you are doing that you are becoming even more relaxed, peaceful, and content."

"Mmmmmmmhh!" articulated my husband.

"And," I continued, "how would it feel if, as you lie there, connecting with your feelings of harmony, relaxation, and inner peace, paying attention to the coolness of the breeze, the aroma of the coffee, the flavours of the food, and the coolness of the sheets, you became aware of a new and different sensation. For between your skin and the sheets, as you continue to enjoy and appreciate the cleanness, the softness, and the coolness of the cotton, you become aware of the irritation caused by thousands and thousands of little tiny toast crumbs."

"Aaaagh!" they both said simultaneously. "You've ruined it. You've spoiled it. How could you do that?" They both moved away from the back of the sofa and started scratching their backs. "That was mean. We were really enjoying that and you spoiled it."

And I replied, "Yes, that's exactly how I feel when I come home and I find the apartment in a mess." And I saw them pause and consider this information.

I can't say they are now perfect in terms of being tidier and more considerate of how I like the apartment to be. But they are much, much better. And I ask myself how this could be. And my conclusion is simply this. In all the years before, I had—of course—spoken Arabic to my husband and son. But this was the first time I had ever **really** spoken to them in **their** language.

Primary source: Sheelagh Deller.

3.08   A Tasty Dish

During the last years of the previous century the President of the United States and his Vice-President were travelling through the state of New Mexico on a fund-raising tour. It was lunchtime, and they were hungry. Finally they reached a small town. There was only one street with a few shops, and there was a diner.

As the men sat down, a waitress came over to the two men and handed them each a menu. The President wasn't sure what to choose. He looked at the menu and then up at the waitress. For five minutes his gaze wavered between both. Finally, he said, "Miss, I think I'll just have a quickie."

The waitress was furious. "I don't care who you are, Mr. President. I'm a well-behaved, God-fearing girl who loves her family and country, and I'm not prepared to take that sort of language from anyone." She stormed off.

The President was speechless.

The Vice-President leaned across the table and said, "With respect, Sir, I think round these parts they pronounce that particular dish **Quiche**."

Primary source: Judith DeLozier.

3.09   *Expert Advice*

When a certain distinguished logician appeared to have died, he was certified dead by physicians and his body prepared for burial. He woke up in the middle of the night on a slab in the mortuary, surrounded by deceased bodies, and, figuring out what had happened, he fainted.

Next day, a long funeral cortège formed to mourn and celebrate the life of the famous man. The mourners passed through the town, chanting, wailing, and beating gongs and drums. At the gates of the cemetery, the noise roused the inhabitant of the coffin to consciousness once again.

He lifted the lid and shouted, "I'm alive, I'm alive. Look, I'm not dead."

But the mourners all said, "Ridiculous, you've been certified dead by medical experts. Death is not the province of logicians."

And so they buried him.

General source: Oriental tradition.

3.10   Information Technomaly

During the early days of the Space Race, the US and the Soviets were desperate to gain the critical edge that would see them first to land a spacecraft on the moon. Prestige, acclamation, and national honour depended upon it.

The key, as it so often is, was the gathering of quality information. The technology had to be refined, and the effects of weightlessness and other non-terrestrial factors on the astronauts explored and understood. Naturally, the astronauts were in the front line of research. They were there, they were living it, so it was essential they kept accurate, experiential, and up to the minute records. This was the ultimate action research project.

However, there was a big problem. When there is no gravity the ink in pens does not flow. Whichever bloc could solve this challenge, it seemed, would win the Space Race. Never before in the history of the world had penmanship been so critical, so essential.

The US government put millions of dollars into funding a project with a well known pen company which developed the pen with a heart, a minipump action that allowed a generation of schoolchildren to write rude messages on classroom ceilings, and US astronauts to make and take critical notes in space.

The Soviets, meanwhile, solved the problem, by giving their astronauts pencils.

Primary source: Ammi Fuller.

3.11 A Triple Punishment

A man well known for his prodigious greed and selfishness was brought before the judge, accused of corruption. The case was clear; the man was manifestly guilty. It only remained for the judge to decide upon the punishment.

The judge, a deeply wise and perceptive woman, considered the nature of the crime and the personality of the man she was dealing with. After a little thought, she looked at the convicted man and said, "I am going to offer you a choice. You may choose your punishment. Choose between these. The first punishment is to pay as a fine a thousand golden dollars. The second is to accept a hundred lashes across your back. The third is to eat ten kilos of raw onions."

The convict was delighted. He could save his money and escape the pain of corporal suffering. "I'll take the onions," he shouted, a huge smile breaking across his face.

However, by the time he had finished just half of the first kilo of raw onions, his eyes were streaming, his thirst was raging, and his stomach felt as if it was going to burst.

"Please," he pleaded, "spare me the onions. I'll take the hundred lashes."

And so it was that the official appointed for this task picked up the lash and began to apply his art to the back of the convict. After no more than ten strokes, the convict could bear the pain no longer. He thought he would die.

"Please," he pleaded, " spare me the lash. I will pay the thousand golden dollars."

And so it was that the convict was punished in each of the three ways for his crime against society, and the judge's insight into character and personality was shown to be profound.

Primary source: Nossrat Peseschkian.
General source: Oriental tradition.

3.12   Wittgenstein

For a quiet and reserved man, it is perhaps not surprising that, among other things, Wittgenstein is celebrated for the following observation:

Whereof one cannot speak, thereof one should not talk.

As a philosopher he is known to have appreciated a piece of advice he was given one day on one of his rare visits to Trinity College, where he was a fellow. Sitting at dinner on top table he was faced with a rather creamy textured and indeterminate pudding.

As he speculatively explored the surface structure of the dessert, a member of the waiting staff leant over and said, "If you dig a little deeper, sir, you'll find a peach." Wittgenstein is said to have considered this as good as any philosophical advice he received while at Cambridge.

Primary source: Thought for the Day, BBC Radio 4 Today programme.

3.13   *Thomas Edison: A strategy for genius*

Thomas Edison took a long time to invent the first light bulb. Rumour has it that he made over 2000 experiments to perfect it.

At the press conference to launch his new invention, a pushy journalist put the knife in:

"Say, Mr Edison, how did it feel to fail to make a light bulb two thousand times?"

"Young man," said Edison, "I didn't fail to make a light bulb two thousand times; I merely found one thousand, nine hundred and ninety nine ways how NOT to make a light bulb."

Primary source: Anecdotal.

3.14   Gary Player

During an important golf tournament, the great golfer Gary Player found himself in a sand trap. A particularly challenging shot was demanded. He rehearsed the shot mentally a couple of times and focused all his powers of concentration. The club kissed the ball sweetly. In a spray of sand, the ball flew into the sky, hung for a moment in the air, descended, bounced twice, and came to rest half a metre from the pin.

As he walked towards the green after the shot, a spectator heckled him from the crowd.

"Hey Gary. That was a really lucky shot."

Gary Player stopped and turned to the man. "I guess you're right," he said. "But you know, it's a funny thing. The more I practice the better I become, and the better I become, the luckier I get."

Primary source: Peter Connolly.

Section 4

Response-ability

Response-ability

"That's a strange sort of a word," said the Young Apprentice. "Response-ability! What sort of a word is that?"

"For historical reasons the English language is very flexible and lends itself well to provocative reformulations that can bend existing meanings and suggest new ones. Such coinages please some and irritate others. Either way it gets their attention.

"This section of the book is about attitude, the ways each of us responds to the different kinds of situations and contexts we can find ourselves in, and how we deal with them. In these situations a lot of choice is open to us, but one major choice is between blaming others for what is happening or taking responsibility ourselves."

"But we can't take responsibility for everything," said the Young One. "That would be ridiculous."

"That is true. The point is, however, that when something happens to you—even if it is outside your control—it is you that will have to live with the consequences, and only you that can deal with it in a way that gets the results you specifically want."

"That sounds quite tough. How does it work in practice?"

"Let me give you an example. Have you ever been in a situation where somebody else assured you of their assistance and support, and then they let you down?"

"Oh yes. That often happens."

"And when it happens, how do you respond?"

"It makes me really angry sometimes. I feel my temperature rise with frustration, I feel tense, and sometimes I even say rude things about the other person. Then I start to feel a bit better."

"True. Blaming someone else can sometimes feel quite cathartic. My question is, how does your behaviour, your anger and frustration, help the situation you are in?"

The question took the Apprentice by surprise. "What? Well ... Umh. It helps me relieve some of my tension. And now I can say if the situation doesn't work out it's not my fault."

"But how does that help you get on usefully with your life and, in particular, change this unwanted or problematic situation into something you do want?"

There was a moment or two of silence. "Not at all, I guess. And, in fact, sometimes I end up feeling bad all day about what has happened and what I've said."

"And how does wasting all that negative energy help the situation? Not one single bit! My young friend, we live in a complex world in which we do not operate alone. Everything we do affects ourselves and others. Everything others do affects themselves and us. We must expect that things will not always work out perfectly, and when situations occur that are not the way we would like, it is simply useful to take responsibility *ourselves* for how we deal with it, because it is we who will have to live with the consequences."

"That sounds hard," the Young Apprentice paused. "But I guess it does make sense."

"It is hard, at first. But once you begin the process of developing response-ability, you may find how easy and liberating it can become. Read the stories in this section, and see if it makes more sense. Only you will know if they ring true."

"So are all these stories about attitude?"

"And what else is concealed below the surface of things also awaits your exploration and discovery."

4.01   *Three Stonemasons*

During the early years of the fourteenth century the foundations of a magnificent cathedral were being laid in central Europe. The Clerk of Works was a monk who was charged with the task of supervising the work of all the labourers and artisans. This monk decided to carry out a study into the working practices of the stonemasons. He singled out three stonemasons as being representative of different attitudes towards their profession.

He approached the first stonemason and said, "My brother, tell me about your work."

The stonemason stopped what he was doing for a moment and replied in a clipped voice full of anger and resentment, "As you see, I sit here in front of my block of stone. It measures a metre, by half a metre, by half a metre. And with every blow of my chisel against the block I feel as if I am chipping away a part of my life. Look, my hands are callused and hard. My face is lined and my hair is grey. This work is never-ending, the same day in, day out. It wears me out. Where's the satisfaction? I'll be dead long before this cathedral is even a quarter finished."

The monk approached the second stonemason. "Brother," he said, "tell me about your work."

"Brother," replied the stonemason in a soft, even voice, "as you see, I sit here in front of my block of stone. It measures a metre, by half a metre, by half a metre. And with every stroke of my chisel against the block I sense that I am carving out a life and a future. Look, how I am able to shelter my family in a comfortable house, far better than that in which I grew up. My children attend school. No doubt they will look forward to even more in life than I do. All this is made possible by my work. As I give to the cathedral through my skill, the cathedral gives to me."

The monk approached the third stonemason. "Brother," he said, "tell me about your work."

"Brother," replied the stonemason smiling and in a voice full of joy, "as you see, I sit here in front of my block of stone. It measures a metre, by half a metre, by half a metre. And with every caress of my chisel against the block I know that I am shaping my destiny. Look, see how the beauty trapped within the form of this stone begins to emerge. Sitting here, I am celebrating not only my craft and the skills of my profession, but am contributing to everything that I value and believe in, a universe—represented by the cathedral—where each gives of his best for the benefit of all. Here at my block I am at peace with who I am, and I am grateful that, although I will never see the completion of this great cathedral, it will still stand a thousand years from now, a beacon celebrating what is truly worthy in all of us, and a testament to the purpose for which the Almighty has put me on this earth."

The monk went away and reflected upon what he had heard. He slept more peacefully that night than he had ever done, and next day he resigned his commission as Clerk of Works and apprenticed himself to the third stonemason.

Primary source: Rachel Naomi Remen, Kitchen Table Wisdom. See bibliography.
Secondary source: Roberto Assagioli.

4.02   *You Have It or You Don't*

A King was watching a great magician perform his act. The crowd were enthralled and so was the King. At the end the audience roared with approval. And the King said: "What a gift this man has. A God-given talent."

But a Wise Counsellor said to the King, "My Lord, genius is made, not born. This magician's skill is the result of discipline and practice. These talents have been learned and honed over time with determination and discipline."

The King was troubled by this message. The Counsellor's challenge had spoiled his pleasure in the magician's arts. "Limited and spiteful swine. How dare you criticise true genius. As I said, you either have it or you don't. And you most certainly don't."

The King turned to his bodyguard and said, "Throw this man into the deepest dungeon. And," he added for the Counsellor's benefit, "so you won't be lonely you can have two of your kind to keep you company. You shall have two piglets as cellmates."

From the very first day of his imprisonment, the Wise Counsellor practised running up the steps of his cell to the prison door carrying in each hand a piglet. As the days turned into weeks, and the weeks into months, the piglets steadily grew into sturdy wild boars. And with every day of practice the Wise Counsellor increased his power and strength.

One day the King remembered the Wise Counsellor and was curious to see how imprisonment had humbled him. He had the Wise Counsellor summoned.

When the prisoner appeared, a man of powerful physique, carrying a wild boar on each arm, the King exclaimed, "What a gift this man has. A God-given talent."

The Wise Counsellor replied, "My Lord, genius is made, not born. My skill is the result of discipline and practice. These talents have been learned and honed over time with determination and discipline."

Primary source: Nossrat Peseschkian.
General source: Oriental tradition.

4.03   *Congruence*

On a certain day in 1456 a farmer entered the great city of Norwich with his son and a donkey. The man was riding the donkey, and his son was leading it on a rope. No sooner had they entered the city walls when they heard a passer-by say in a loud voice, "How disgraceful. See how that man sits on his donkey behaving like a lord of the manor while his little son runs himself ragged trying to keep up." Full of shame, the farmer dismounted and set his son on the donkey while he walked beside it.

In the next street, a peddler drew his customer's attention to the trio. "Look at that. That little rascal sits up there like the Young Pretender while his poor old father trudges along in the mud." Deeply embarrassed, the boy asked his father to climb on behind him.

Once they turned the corner into the next street, a woman selling bat legs and toad venom spat out, "See what has become of the human race. No sensitivity to animals. Look at that poor donkey. Its back's almost bent in two carrying the weight of those two loafers. If only I had my wand with me … disgraceful!"

Hearing this the farmer and his son without a word slipped off the donkey and began to walk beside it. They hadn't gone more than fifty yards, however, when they heard a market-stall holder shout across the market to his friend, "I thought I was stupid but look, here's a real ass. What's the point of having a donkey when it doesn't do any donkey work?"

The farmer stopped, and having given his donkey a pat on the nose, said to his son, "Whatever we do, someone disagrees with it. Perhaps it's time we made up our own minds about what we believe is right."

Primary source: Mark Richards.
General source: Oriental tradition. There is a version in Idries Shah.

4.04   Not Yet Ready

Zeus and Hera were gazing down from the Heavens, observing the plight of humankind. Hera was particularly upset by a poor man, burdened down by the weight of his troubles, his hunger, and the demands of his family, whom he could neither feed nor humour.

"My Lord," she said to Zeus, "Be compassionate. Send help to that poor man there. See, he is so poor, that his sandals are tied together with seaweed."

"My Love," replied Zeus, "I would gladly help him, but he is not yet ready."

"Shame on you," retorted Hera. "It would be the easiest thing in the world for you to cast down on the path in front of him a sack of gold to ease all his worries for ever."

"Aaah! Now that is another thing entirely," said the Master of the Universe.

A vivid bolt of lightning, accompanied by a huge crack of thunder, rent the cloudless sky. The world seemed to stop for a moment and then the birds resumed their singing and the cicadas their sawing.

A sack containing gold of the purest quality lay on the path in front of the poor man who carefully lifted his feet and stepped over it in order not to damage his sandals further.

Primary source: Kiki Stamigou.
Secondary source: There is a version in Sue Knight, NLP Solutions. See bibliography.

4.05   The Grammarian

A Businessman had invited his friend the Schoolmaster for a trip on his boat. It was a hot day, and while the Businessman attended to the steering and navigation, the Schoolmaster relaxed on the deck.

After a while, the Schoolmaster asked, "What will the weather be like?"

The Businessman looked at the sky, sniffed the air, and checked the direction of the wind.

"We's going to have a storm," he said.

The Schoolmaster was shocked. "You can't say 'We's'! Don't you know grammar? You should say, '*We're* … We're going to have a storm.' My friend, if you don't know grammar you've wasted half your life."

The Businessman merely shrugged his shoulders and carried on navigating the boat with skill and an eye on the horizon.

Some time later, as the Businessman had predicted, a huge storm blew up. The wind was high, the waves were huge, and the little boat was swamped with water.

Over the roar of the storm, the Businessman shouted to the Schoolmaster, "Have you ever learned how to swim?"

"No. Why on earth should I have learned to swim?"

"In that case," said the Businessman grinning from ear to ear, "you've wasted all your life, because we's going to sink."

Primary source: Nossrat Peseschkian. See bibliography.
General source: Oriental tradition.

A slightly different version of this story appeared in New Standpoints Magazine, November 2000, Paris.

4.06   Buried Treasure

Many years ago—and it wasn't my time, and it wasn't your time, but it was somebody's time—there lived, in a remote part of Wales, a young man. He was a shepherd and spent his days and nights looking after the few sheep that he had inherited from his parents before they died.

He was very poor, for the sheep brought him little income. He had barely enough to eat and clothe himself with. But he had his dreams. Dreams of a successful future, in which he saw himself studying at a great seat of learning, and using his knowledge to make a great impression on the world. He dreamed of a world in which all young people would have an opportunity to go to school and study in order to improve the quality of their lives and multiply their opportunities. Just as he himself longed to do.

And although he very much loved the sheep in his care, the beauty of the countryside, the passing of the seasons, and the joy of waking each new day, he sensed there was more to life than this. And somehow he knew that to achieve what he wanted he would somehow have to make his own fortune.

In the summer months he would spend much of his time in the high pastures of the Welsh hills where it was quiet and solitary. Often he would sleep in the ruins of an abandoned chapel, curling up beside the stone walls, sheltering under what remained of the roof, and protected from the weather by the leaves of a great oak tree that had, many years before, seeded itself in the floor of the old church, and now spread its huge branches and leaf canopy above and beyond the confines of the ruined walls.

One night, as he slept here, the boy had a dream. And the dream too planted a seed. In his dream the boy dreamed that a strange figure, robed from head to foot in white and green, had come to him and said, "Why do you remain here? If you wish to live your dream, wake up! Do not wait for the world to give you what you seek. Take action! What you want, you must seek. Go to London. On London Bridge your fortune waits. That's where you'll find it. Go seek."

And the acorn in his mind began to grow, and he sold his sheep, saying goodbye solemnly to each one, and began to plan the long walk to London. He took with him sheep's cheese to taste, and pure Welsh spring water to drink, and with the freshness of the upland smells in his clothes and hair, he set off. He crossed wide valleys and roaring rivers, he skirted sprawling cities and hiked high hills, he traced the tracks of traders, always heading south and east, until finally he arrived at the great metropolis of London Town.

Now, in those days, London Bridge was rather different than it is today. It had many, many arches, and on each side of the bridge, all the way across the river, were shops and houses. The bridge was crowded, bristling with all kinds of life. There were merchants standing in the doorways of their shops shouting their wares. There were horses and carts bringing people and animals to and from the market, the rich passing by in their carriages, and the poor passing by on foot, peering into shop windows at things they couldn't afford. All the world was there, in all its richness. The sights, smells, and sounds of bustling city life.

The young shepherd arrived one day at noon. He had never seen so much activity, or heard so much noise, or felt such excitement in his life. But he was on a mission to find his fortune, so he walked along the length of the bridge to find his destiny. And then he walked back to find where he might have missed it. And returned again. And back again. Time and again, all afternoon and evening, searching for what he could not find. He searched long into the night, even after everybody had long gone home, until, exhausted, he finally slumped down in a shop doorway and slept.

He dreamed of his sheep that now he very much missed …

Until he got woken rudely at six in the morning by a sharp kick in the ribs. "Oi! Get up you little bastard," roared the merchant whose doorway the shepherd had slept in. "Whatch'up ter? I been watchin' ya'll yes'day art'noon'n'evenin'. Whatch'up ter? Walkin' up 'n down. Nosein' in at all the shops. Lookin' at cracks in the pavin' stones. Wondrin' what might fall off the back o' the carts. I've a good mind ter turn y'over to the law. Wha's yer game, son?"

109

"I came here to look for my fortune," stammered the shepherd. "I had a dream."

The merchant rolled his eyes. A small crowd had gathered. "You'll have to do better 'an that, sunshine. Tell us about this dream o' yours, then."

The shepherd explained about the stranger in the white and green robe. "He told me I'd find my fortune here on London Bridge. So I came here all the way from Wales, sold all my sheep see, to find it."

The merchant roared with laughter. "Pay no attention to dreams. Dreams are for fools, children, old women, and priests. Take my advice, get a proper job, and get on with your life. Work and destiny; that's what matters. Now, move on."

"But my dream ..."

"Listen," cut in the merchant. "Dreams are waste of space. They're just the Devil's work. I had a dream meself last night ... but I'd as soon cut my own throat as take any notice of it. Let me see now. There I was, on a high Welsh hillside, and there was an old ruined church, made of stone and with no roof, and in the middle of that ruin there grew an enormous tree. An oak tree. And there I see, buried deep under the soil, between the roots of that vast oak, a chest of treasure, hidden in haste long ago by a one-eyed pirate. Hah! It's just a dream, a childish fantasy. That's all. Nothing more."

But the young shepherd had already gone, heading back north and west to the Welsh hills. Heading back towards the land of his fathers, towards the sweet smelling pastures of the uplands he had left behind so many weeks ago. And it wasn't long before he started digging.

* * *

The shepherd never did go to a seat of learning, but he did something else instead. He used his fortune, the pirate's treasure, profitably, and in time became a wealthy merchant, the richest in those parts. And with his profits he built schools, he attracted the best teachers, he offered scholarships for the poor. And it wasn't long before that particular part of his native land had as rich and diverse a culture as any other place in the kingdom.

Today you can still find his statue at the centre of the town where he built his first seat of learning for the poor and underprivileged. On the pedestal are written the words:

> Follow your dream
> And seek it out
> Your fortune may be closer than you think
> Notice all that is around you
> For it is all there to serve you
> Do not dismiss an acorn
> However small
> For the acorn is father to the oak

Primary sources: Hugh Lupton, Paolo Coelho, Sufi tradition.
Secondary source: Paolo Coelho, The Alchemist. See bibliography.

4.07 The Flood

Right in the heart of America is a very famous town. It's famous for several reasons. Firstly, because it's right smack in the geographical centre of the continental landmass. Secondly, because it's a town of extremes: it's either very, very hot or very, very cold; either very, very wet or very, very dry; either very, very windy or very, very still.

Just to the north are high mountains, where the water collects as rainfall or snow to form the river which runs right through the heart of the town.

Now, I don't know if you read about this place recently in the newspapers, or saw it on TV, or heard about it on the radio, but there was a major crisis there a few weeks ago.

Rain started up there in the mountains. Heavy rain, ceaseless rain. It rained for days, and the river got higher and higher until it burst its banks. And the authorities got worried so they sent in buses to evacuate all the people. Everybody left on the buses except a few who refused to leave their homes saying the crisis would pass.

Among these was an old man whose views were particularly strong. "I'm not leaving here," he told the authorities, "this is my town, this is my home, and anyway I trust in God, I have faith in God, I believe in God. God will save me. I ain't going nowhere!"

And so the authorities and their buses left.

And it continued raining and raining and raining. And the river got higher and higher and higher. Until, by the middle of the next day, the water was half way up all the houses. All the folks who had remained were leaning out of their first floor windows waiting for help.

Now the authorities were really worried so they sent boats to rescue all the people. And all the people were taken to safety.

Except this one old man.

"I'm not leaving here, this is my town, this is my home, and anyway I trust in God, I have faith in God, I believe in God. God will save me. I ain't going nowhere!"

And so the authorities and their boats left.

And it continued raining and raining and raining. And the river got higher and higher and higher. Until by the middle of the next day the water was lapping at the tip of the rooftops. And there sat the old man on top of his roof with one leg on side and one leg on the other.

And now the authorities were really really worried so they sent a helicopter to rescue the old man. And it flew in low, flattening all the water around, frightening all the birds with its chugging and chopping noise, and from a door at the side of the helicopter a man was lowered down on a rope.

"Jump! Jump! I'll save you," said the rescuer.

But the old man was adamant and waved the helicopter away.

"I'm not leaving here, this is my town, this is my home, and anyway I trust in God, I have faith in God, I believe in God. God will save me. I ain't going nowhere!"

And so the authorities and their helicopter left.

And it continued raining and raining and raining. And the river got higher and higher and higher. Until …

Well, to cut a long story short, the old man drowned …

And his soul went up to the place where souls go. And he was angry. He was really really angry. He had been let down! Big time! To have had all that faith and trust! For what?

He hammered on the Gate, waking up any inside who might have been asleep. The huge wooden Gate slowly swung open on its hinges with a loud creak. Immediately the old man demanded to see God. "I got a bone to pick with God. I wanna see him right now. He let me down. Big time!"

Now, Saint Peter, the one who looked after all the traffic coming through the Gate, had all manner of qualifications in understanding human behaviour. "OK, OK," he said, picking up the anger and frustration in the old man's voice, "I can see how angry you feel, and I have to say if I was looking at things from your point of view I'd probably feel the same."

"Cut the flannel," said the old man, "I want to see God and I want to see him right now. I wanna give him a piece of my mind."

"OK, OK. I'll see what I can do," said Saint Peter, picking up the hotline to the Penthouse. "Hello God, sorry to trouble you, but I've got a guy down here who says you let him down. He's real angry and says he has a bone to pick with you. What shall I do?"

"Send him right on up," said God.

Saint Peter put the old man in the celestial elevator and punched the penthouse button. The lift shot upwards. After what seemed an eternity, the doors opened and the old man found himself face to face with God.

Once again he exploded into anger. "God, I've got a big bone to pick with you. How could you do this to me? You let me down. I trusted in you, I had faith in you, I believed in you. I thought you would save me. And you let me down. Big time!"

God remained calm and gazed steadily at the man. When the old man had finished, God simply said, "What do you mean 'I let you down'? Have you not learned to use the gifts I gave you: your five senses, your brain, and all the resources in the world around you?"

"What the hell are you talking about?" demanded the old man.

"First I sent you buses, then I sent you boats, and finally I sent you a helicopter. In your next life you will do well to take a little more responsibility for yourself."

Primary source: Julian Russell.

4.08   Faith

A devout merchant drove his Mercedes hundreds of miles across the Arabian deserts to worship with a Holy Man. When he arrived he parked his car outside the simple lodging and entered to embark on a week of study. He fasted, meditated, and prayed for seven days and nights, fully surrendering himself to the power of almighty God.

But when he looked for his car afterwards, he discovered it was no longer where he had left it. He searched everywhere, but his Mercedes was nowhere to be seen. He complained bitterly to the Holy Man. "Look how I have been let down. I have spent days and nights worshipping, and see how God treats me!"

The Holy Man smiled and said: "Trust in God *and* tie your camel securely."

General source: Oriental tradition.

4.09   The Spoons

There was a woman who died. Her soul left her body and floated up to Heaven. She knocked at the gate of the archangel. It was a huge solid wooden door, and when it opened it creaked on its ancient rusty hinges.

When the archangel saw the woman, he took a large intake of breath and said: "So you've finally come. We've been dreading your arrival."

"What do you mean," said the woman, "dreading my arrival?"

"Well," said the archangel, "you know it's my job to direct people to Heaven or Hell. The problem is that in your case we just don't know what to do with you."

"What do you mean, don't know what to do with me?"

"Well," replied the archangel, "you know we have scales for these matters, a huge set of scales upon which we place all the good you've done on one side, and all the bad on the other. Whichever side is heavier decides whether you will go up to Heaven or down to Hell."

"So?"

"In your case, and this is our problem, when we weigh your life the scales are exactly balanced. It's never happened before. We don't know what to do with you."

"Don't know what to do with me!! Where am I going to go, then? What are you going to do about it?"

"We thought we'd let you choose."

The woman was stunned for a moment. "Me choose? You're joking, aren't you? Me choose whether I go to Heaven or Hell?"

"Yes," said the archangel.

There was a long pause. Finally the woman asked: "What's the difference; what's the difference between the two?"

"Between Heaven and Hell? There is no material difference, none, none at all," replied the Keeper of the Gate.

"None? NONE AT ALL? You're joking!"

"No, no I'm not. This is not a joking matter. We want you to choose which place you'd like to make your eternal home."

There was another long pause. Finally the woman said, "Are you sure there's no difference?"

"Well," said the archangel, "would you like to see for yourself and then make up your mind?" The woman nodded. "Where would you like to start? Up or Down?"

"I think Up," she said.

"Fine. Now we're talking of big places here, where do you want to start?" The woman looked puzzled. "Let me help you. What were your passions while you were alive?"

"Oh, that's easy. Food and drink."

"So shall we start with the restaurant, then?"

The woman nodded and together they entered the celestial elevator. The Celestial Restaurant was many floors up. Even before the elevator doors opened the woman could smell the delicious aromas, smells that brought a sense of joy and abandonment to her whole being. When the doors opened she saw long tables, covered with plain white cloths, and simple benches on either side. On the benches sat rows of relaxed friendly looking people, smiling, well fed, and chatting amiably to each other.

On the tables themselves were large silver tureens containing soup from which the delicious aromas were emanating. She became aware of her desire to eat, to taste the food that smelt so wonderful.

She noticed the sense of space willing to be filled in the centre of herself, and the presence of saliva in her mouth.

And then she noticed something unusual. There was no cutlery on the table, neither forks nor knives, no teaspoons or dessert spoons, only very long silver serving spoons. But these spoons were huge; each one was at least a metre and a half in length.

The archangel asked her opinion. "Wonderful," she said, "but now I'm curious to look at the other place to see for myself if it really is the same."

Down they went in the Infernal Elevator. She was surprised to notice no difference in either pressure or temperature. Even before the elevator doors opened at the Infernal Restaurant the woman could smell the same delicious aromas as she'd experienced in the Celestial Restaurant, smells that brought the same sense of joy and abandonment to her whole being. When the doors opened she saw long tables, covered with plain white cloths, and simple benches on either side, just as before.

On the tables here were also large silver tureens containing soup from which the delicious aromas were emanating. She became aware once again of her desire to eat, to taste the food that smelled so wonderful. She noticed the same sense of space willing to be filled in the centre of herself, and the presence of saliva in her mouth.

And she noticed the same unusual situation with the cutlery: neither forks nor knives, no teaspoons nor dessert spoons, only the very long silver serving spoons each one at least a metre and a half in length.

And then she noticed that there was a difference. She had been so taken with the smells of the food, the elegant simplicity of the dining arrangements, and the curiosity of the cutlery that she hadn't noticed the silence and baleful atmosphere. On the benches sat rows of people, sitting opposite each other as in the Celestial Restaurant. But whereas those in Heaven were relaxed, friendly looking people, smiling, well fed, and chatting amiably to each other, these were completely different.

These people were sullen and baleful, staring meanly and suspiciously at each other. And even though the soup in the tureens was as plentiful on these tables as it was in the Heavenly restaurant, these people looked starved and emaciated, as if they hadn't eaten for weeks.

The woman turned to the Keeper of the Gate. "In every respect except the people the restaurants in Heaven and Hell are the same. Yet here even though there is plenty the people are starving and angry. What is the difference that makes the difference?"

The archangel said: "Yes, I mentioned to you that there is no *material* difference. I neglected to mention attitude. The difference is in people's *attitude*. You have seen the spoons. The simple fact is that down here in Hell the people try to feed themselves. Up there in Heaven, the people take pleasure in feeding each other."

Primary source: Anecdotal.
General sources: There are many versions of this story.

4.10   Heaven and Hell

The old King was sick and feared death. He summoned his Fool to prepare him for a transition to the land from which no traveller returns.

"What's the difference between Heaven and Hell?" he demanded.

"What can you know of these subtle things?" responded the Fool. "All you know is military campaigns, rape, pillage, and the oppression of your subjects. You're too old, stupid, and impotent to know about subtlety."

Hearing these words, the King flew into a great rage and summoned his bodyguard to arrest the Fool. On the orders of the King the Fool was stripped, whipped, and stretched on the rack. But the Fool remained impassive as if torture was no concern of his. The Fool's inner calmness infuriated the King even more. And in his rage he grabbed a broadsword and was just about to cleave the Fool from nonce to navel when a smile in the eyes of the Fool stopped him in his tracks.

"Now you know what Hell is," said the Fool, holding steadily in his gaze the eyes of the King.

"You risked your life to show me that?" said the King incredulously. "You were whipped and tortured to within an inch of your life, and yet you were unmoved. You smiled at me when I was about to introduce your brains to your guts. You had no fear of death?"

"Well, that is Heaven," said the Fool.

Primary source: Anecdotal.
Secondary source: There is a version in Sue Knight, NLP Solutions. See bibliography.

4.11   Hot Buttons

Mole was driving along a motorway with his friend, Badger. Mole was enjoying the drive and feeling good about the world until another car, driven by Rat, cut aggressively and dangerously in front of him.

Mole was furious. He put his foot on the accelerator and chased after Rat, flashing, hooting, and gesticulating. Mole was shouting and cursing, and purple with rage. Rat simply laughed to himself, made a rude gesture with his fingers, and accelerated away.

Mole was quite upset for the next hour. His day was totally spoilt. He felt frustrated and inadequate, as if his whole sense of masculinity had been called into question. He had been challenged and come off second-best.

Badger had noticed his friend's behaviour but had chosen to say nothing for the time being. He waited until the time was right.

Finally Mole turned and said to him, "That sort of driver makes me so angry."

Badger replied, "Forgive me, but I'm really curious. How exactly do you allow yourself to get angry because of what another driver does?"

Mole was speechless. He had expected support. "What do you mean?"

Badger said, "What that other person did was simply information about him. How you responded is information about you. How exactly did you *make yourself* angry as a response to the other driver's behaviour?"

And so it was that Mole began to realise that he could choose his response to different situations. He could get angry if he wished, or stay calm and dismiss someone else's behaviour as information about them. It didn't have to affect him.

After that Mole began to enjoy his driving a lot more. Badger felt a lot safer in Mole's car, and Mole's wife noticed her husband was much less stressed and aggressive.

One day Mole told Badger that he'd found a great quote in a book he was reading.

"No one presses your hot buttons. You just leave your control panel open."

"That's what I used to do," Mole said, stressing the *used to*.

Contributing source: The hot buttons quote is in: Righting the Educational Conveyor Belt by Michael Grinder. See bibliography.

4.12   Assumptions

Two cars were being driven fast and in opposite directions along a winding country lane. It was late summertime, and the hedgerows on either side of the lane were lush and high. It was impossible to see around any of the corners.

Both drivers, because of the heat of the day, had their windows wound down, and their minds were focused on the road ahead and their destination. And, as it happened, the driver of one of the cars was a man and the other was a woman.

They approached the final bend at speed, and they only just managed to see each other in time. They stood on their brakes, and just managed to slide past each other without scraping the paintwork.

As they did so, the woman turned to the man, and through the open window she shouted: "PIG!"

Quick as a flash he replied: "COW!"

He accelerated around the corner … and crashed into a pig.

Primary source: Rabbi Lionel Blue on Thought for the Day, BBC Radio 4 Today programme.

4.13   Service

The Magician was running a course. The group was a challenging one. There were different value systems and agendas at work. Some wanted one thing, others something else. Some thought they were superior to others on the programme, in knowledge and sophistication, and that the others were slowing them down. Some thought certain people were arrogant, demanding, and selfish. Everybody thought the training room was too small. Once somebody develops an itch, everybody wants one. And then it spreads.

The Magician waited, hoping that the dynamic of the group would resolve itself. It didn't. She went home for the weekend and considered her strategic options. There were many, but certainly some would work better than others.

Breaking off from her strategic thinking she opened her mail that had accumulated in her mailbox during the week. From a large brown envelope she took a glossy promotional brochure for a training programme and idly glanced through it.

Attending to a section headed "Notes for Delegates", she was struck, as she had so often been before, by the remarkable fact that the world is there to serve us if only we will notice. She read the section carefully and knew what she would do.

On Monday morning, in a new and larger room, she wrote on the flipchart in large letters:

How can I be of service ...

>   *To myself?*
>   *To others?*
>   *To the trainer?*

How can a Magician be of service ...

>   *To herself?*
>   *To each and every member of the group?*

How can each and every one of us be a magician, an agent of transformation, to ourselves and to others?

And she added as a footnote a quote of Aldous Huxley.

'Experience isn't what happens to us. It's what we do with what happens to us.'

There was a long and quiet moment of reflection. And as the message was understood, the process of transforming began.

Contributing source: The advice on 'Service' was found in a John Seymour Associates' pamphlet: Advice to Training Assistants.

4.14   *The Chicken and the Eagle*

There was a chicken farmer who was a very keen rock climber. One day, climbing a particularly challenging rock face, he came upon a large ledge. On the ledge was a large nest and in the nest, three large eggs. Eagle eggs.

He knew it was distinctly unecological, and undoubtedly illegal, but temptation got the better of him and he discreetly put one of the eagle eggs in his rucksack, checking first to make sure the mother eagle wasn't around. Then he continued his climb, drove back to his ranch, and put the eagle egg in the hen house.

That night the mother hen sat on the huge egg, the proudest chicken you ever saw. And the cock seemed pretty pleased with himself too.

In the fullness of time the egg hatched and the baby eagling emerged. It looked around and saw the mother hen. "Mama!" it squawked.

And so it was that the eagle grew up with its brother and sister chicks. It learned to do all the things that chickens do: clucking and cackling, scratching in the dirt for grits and worms, flapping its wings furiously, and flying a few feet into the air before crashing to earth in a pile of dust and feathers. And believing above all things that it was totally and absolutely a chicken.

One day late in its life, the eagle-who-thought-he-was-a-chicken happened to look up at the sky. High overhead, soaring majestically on the thermal currents, flying effortlessly with scarcely a beat of its powerful golden wings, was an eagle.

"What's that?" said the old eagle in awe to his farmyard neighbour. "It's magnificent. So much power and grace. Poetry in motion."

"That's an eagle," said the chicken. "That's the King of the Birds. It's a bird of the air. But we, we're only chickens, we're birds of the earth."

And so it was that the eagle lived and died a chicken; because that's all it thought it was.

Primary source: Fr. Anthony de Mello SJ, quoted in Awareness, Fount.

4.15 Marriage Bans

In the café a man was listening to his friend with a certain amount of envy. "I can't begin to tell you," said the friend, "just how wonderful it is to have two women in one's life. Since I married my second wife I have begun to experience the joys of variety. Just as a ruby and an emerald please the eye in different ways, and each flower produces its own pleasing aroma, just so it is to enrich my life in this way."

The man thought to himself that his friend must be living in Paradise. He felt the sting of envy and the desire to taste the sweetness of different fruit.

So it was that some weeks later he married a second wife. But when he arrived at her bedchamber on the first evening of the marriage he got short shrift. "Leave me in peace and let me sleep," she shouted at him. "Go to your first wife. I'm not going to be your bit on the side. Make your choice: her or me."

When he arrived at his first wife's bedroom another unpleasant surprise awaited him. "Don't think I'm going to entertain you here. If I'm so little use to you that you need a second whore, don't think to show your face around here. Go back to her."

The poor man had no choice but to look for somewhere to sleep at the mosque. He knelt down in a praying position and tried to sleep. But try as he might sleep would not come. However, after a short while he was disturbed by a polite cough behind him. He turned around and much to his surprise saw his friend that had the two wives.

"What are you doing here?" he asked his friend, amazed.

The friend explained he had been having trouble with his two wives for quite a long time.

"So why on earth did you tell me how marvellous it was to enjoy the company of two women?"

Shamefaced, the friend confessed that he had been so lonely spending every evening at the mosque that he had felt a desperate need for company.

Primary source: Nossrat Peseschkian.
General source: Oriental tradition.

Section 5

Choice Changes

Choice Changes

"I'm confused about this title," confessed the Apprentice. "Does it mean that having a choice enables people to make changes, or allows people to become changed, or does it mean that the stories in this section offer quality changes for the better, like choice cuts of meat, or does it mean something else entirely?"

"Language can indeed be slippery and ambiguous. I'm reading a novel at the moment called 'Enduring Love': what do you suppose that means?"

"But isn't it better if meaning is clear, straightforward, and unambiguous?"

"Sometimes it needs to be. And in those situations it is quite an art to ensure that it is. At other times it is also artful to be ambiguous in order to create space for others to make their own connections and supply their own answers—now, that too would be useful, isn't it?"

The Young Apprentice felt he hadn't quite grasped the gist of this last statement.

"The important thing," the Magician added, "is to choose consciously whether you wish to be straightforward or whether you wish to be ambiguous, and for what purpose."

To cover his confusion, the Apprentice returned to firmer ground. "So what exactly *is* this section about?"

"That," the Magician replied deliberately, "is a hard question. It seems to me to be about many things including making choices and making changes, and about creating the choices and changes that we want to happen in our lives."

"Why is it so hard to pin you down sometimes? You're supposed to be a magician!"

"What leads you to suppose that magicians know all the answers?"

The Apprentice pondered a moment on his own frustration and temerity. "Sorry. I didn't choose my words very well."

The Magician smiled. "Nor your tone. And you're right, it is usually useful to behave as if more choice is better than no choice. If you have only one way of doing things that is no choice at all. If you have two ways of doing something that is a dilemma. You need *at least* three ways of acting in any situation to have a real sense of choice, and so that you can get the results you want for yourself and for others." The Magician paused. "What do you learn from this?" she asked.

The Apprentice thought hard for a moment or two. "I guess every situation is different and every person is unique. So it's important to choose our responses carefully so they are appropriate to the people involved and the contexts in which the interactions are taking place."

"Precisely. There is a useful three-step model for taking action so that you make the right choices in order to get the changes you want. First, you need to know what *result* you want to get from any situation, both for yourself and for any others who are involved. Second, *be aware* of the responses you are getting from these other people as you interact with them. Pay attention to the information they give you not only through the words they use, but also—and more importantly—through the vocal tone and nonverbal communication with which they express their real and underlying meaning. Finally—and this is where having plenty of choices in how you respond is important—*behave flexibly* in order to ensure you are moving towards the results you want and not away from them."

"Aha! Of course. That's your old message that if what I'm doing isn't working, it's a good idea to do something different. And so this is how having more choices will help me get the changes I want in my life."

"Unless you are being chased by an angry bull, in which case I would recommend that you ignore choice and just run as fast as you can."

"But I guess I could still choose the most useful direction?"

"Precisely."

5.01   *The Jam Jar*

The Mullah's wife was planning to make baklava, a dish prepared with nuts. The Mullah was particularly fond of baklava, especially when it contained a lot of nuts, so he went to the cellar to bring his wife plenty of nuts from the jar.

He shoved his hand deep into the bottom of the jar and grasped as many nuts as he could get his fingers around. But when he attempted to extract his hand, he found to his dismay that it had become stuck fast in the neck of the jar. No matter how hard he pulled he could not release his arm from the tenacious grip of the jar's mouth.

He shouted and hollered for help. He uttered many oaths and curses, which, of course, mullahs are not really supposed to do. His wife arrived and together they tried everything they could think of doing but still the jar would not release his arm.

Neighbours were summoned, but in spite of all their ideas nothing succeeded in achieving the desired result and the Mullah's hand remained firmly clamped in the mouth of the jar.

A passing traveller, attracted by the commotion and the whimpering sighs of the Mullah, asked what had happened. The Mullah told him of the steps that had led to his imprisonment.

"If you promise to do everything I tell you," said the traveller, "I can help."

The Mullah agreed. "I'll do whatever you say. Just free me from this confounded jar."

"Then shove your arm further in."

The Mullah thought this was a ridiculous thing to do as he wanted to get his hand out. But he reluctantly did as he had promised to do.

"Now open your fingers and let go of the nuts. All of them."

This instruction was hardly what the Mullah wanted to hear. After all he needed the nuts for the baklava his wife was going to prepare for him. But again he reluctantly did so.

"Now make your hand long and slender and gently slide it out of the jar."

To the Mullah's amazement, and the appreciative cries of the onlookers, the hand slipped easily out of the jar.

But the Mullah continued to be exercised about the situation. "This is all very well, and I'm pleased to regain the freedom of my hand, but what about the nuts I need for the baklava?"

The traveller took the jar, tipped it to one side, and let as many nuts as the Mullah needed spill out onto the table.

The Mullah was astonished. He looked at the traveller with wonder and deep respect and asked, "Are you a Magician?"

Primary source: Nossrat Peseschkian.
General source: Oriental tradition.

5.02   *The Monk and the Thief*

A thief was watching a very holy monk through a crack in the monastery door. The monk was polishing some heavy antique candlesticks made of the finest gold. As he watched, the monk, needing some more rags, turned around and walked straight through a thick stone wall into the next room to fetch some. The thief was amazed and realised that here was a skill that would give him an advantage.

The thief entered the monastery and said to the monk, "Master, will you teach me to walk through walls?"

"That I will," said the monk. "But you will have to become my pupil and do everything exactly as I ask you. Then you will learn to walk through walls."

The thief agreed and did everything exactly as the monk asked. After a year, the thief approached the monk and said, "Master, I have not yet learned to walk through walls."

The monk replied, "Be patient, my son. If you do everything exactly as I ask you, then you will learn to walk through walls."

After five more years, doing exactly as the monk instructed him, the thief again approached the monk and said, "Master, I have not yet learned to walk through walls."

The monk replied, "Be patient, my son. If you do everything exactly as I ask you, then you will learn to walk through walls."

After ten more years, doing exactly as the monk instructed him, the thief again approached the monk and said, "Master, I have not yet learned to walk through walls."

The monk replied, "Be patient, my son. If you do everything exactly as I ask you, then you will learn to walk through walls."

One day the monk instructed the thief to fetch him some rags to polish the candlesticks.

The thief walked straight through the thick stone wall into the next room to fetch some.

He didn't even notice.

Primary source: Jane Revell & Susan Norman, Handing Over. See bibliography.

5.03   Cutting Remarks

You may have seen it on TV, or heard about it on the radio, or read about it in the newspaper, but recently the annual World Logging Championship was held in British Columbia. The two finalists were a Canadian and a Norwegian.

Their task was straightforward. Each had a sector of the forest. Whoever could fell the most timber between 8 o'clock in the morning and 4 o'clock in the afternoon would be the winner.

At 8 o'clock sharp, the whistle blew and the two lumberjacks set to with attitude. It seemed that they chopped stroke for stroke until at ten to nine the Canadian heard the Norwegian stop. Sensing his chance, the Canadian redoubled his efforts.

At 9 o'clock the Canadian heard the Norwegian start chopping again. Once more it seemed as if they chopped stroke for stroke until at ten to ten the Canadian heard the Norwegian stop. Again the Canadian continued, determined to make the most of his opponent's weakness.

At the stroke of 10 o'clock, the Norwegian began cutting again. Until at ten to eleven, the Norwegian paused once more. With a growing sense of confidence, the Canadian scented victory, and continued in his steady rhythm.

And so it went on throughout the whole day. Every hour at ten to the hour, the Norwegian would stop and the Canadian would continue. When the whistle blew to finish the contest at 4 o'clock in the afternoon, the Canadian was supremely confident that the prize was his.

You can imagine how surprised he was to discover that he had lost.

"How did you do that?" he asked the Norwegian. "Every hour at ten to the hour I heard you stop. How the hell were you able to cut more timber than me? It's just not possible."

"It's really very simple," said the Norwegian bluntly. "Every hour, at ten to the hour, I stopped. While you continued to cut, I was sharpening my axe."

Primary source: Anecdotal.

5.04   *Pebbles*

The three nomads were preparing to sleep. It was pitch black in the middle of the desert and getting cold. They had parked their camels, taken what they needed from the saddle bags, pitched their tents, and rolled out their sleeping mats. They were just about to settle down for the night when their attention was attracted to a curious glowing light on the horizon.

As they watched, the light brightened. It gained intensity, it gleamed and glowed and glistened, galloping towards them, until it filled the whole of the night sky. And they knew, each one absolutely knew, they were in the presence of some kind of Divine Being, and they waited for the words which they knew would come.

And the words came.

And the words said: "Go forth into the desert. Gather as many pebbles as you can. And tomorrow will find you delighted, disappointed, and very, very curious …"

And that was it. There was no more. Only silence.

And the light receded back from where it had come, until all was dark again except for the twinkling of the stars high in the black night.

And the nomads were furious.

"What kind of God is this?" demanded one. "Gather pebbles? Who does He think we are? Menials? Rubbish collectors? I belong to a proud race. That I should stoop so low!"

Another added: "Now a real God would have done things differently. A real God would have shared secrets with us. Would have told us how to eradicate poverty and suffering; or how to prevent global warming; or how to irrigate the desert."

"A real God," said the third, "would have given us the key to success; given us the winning lottery numbers; shown us how to become rich and famous."

But perhaps because of their memory of the purity of the light, or the resonant authority of the voice that spoke the words, the nomads went out into the desert, still grumbling and complaining, perfunctorily gathered a few pebbles, and threw them grudgingly into the depths of their saddlebags.

And then they went to bed.

The next morning dawned fine. The nomads rolled up their sleeping mats, dismantled their tents, stowed them in their saddlebags, and set off for the next oasis. They rode with the sun arcing high overhead, across steep dunes and through deep rocky canyons. They rode all day until, as the sun sank in the west, they saw its reflection glinting on the lake at the centre of the oasis they sought.

And they went through the ritual they went through every day. They parked the camels. They pitched their tents. They unrolled their sleeping mats.

And then, one of the nomads went over to look for something in his saddlebag. And as he rummaged around his hand closed on something small, round, and hard. A pebble. And when he pulled it out, and to his amazement discovered it was a diamond, he couldn't believe it. And he searched for, and pulled out the others, calling to his companions, and they too found that all their pebbles had become diamonds.

And you can imagine how delighted they were.

Until they realised how few they had collected the previous evening. And you can imagine how disappointed they were.

But after a while they got to thinking about the meaning of all this. These pebbles, which the previous night they had considered so worthless, were now precious. And they began to wonder how many other things in their lives, things that they had previously considered of little or no consequence in the past, might have a value that they hadn't discovered or considered yet.

And they began to get more and more curious about discovering meanings, under the surface of things, which now they were beginning dimly to apprehend with growing excitement and wonder.

Primary source: Christina Hall.
Secondary source: There is a version of this story in Jack Canfield & Mark Victor Hansen, Chicken Soup for the Soul, Volume 2. See bibliography.

5.05   *The Watermelon*

A traveller was crossing a broad and barren plain. He'd been travelling since morning and now he was hot, tired, and hungry. He watched the sun setting towards the mountains in the west and began wondering where he might find a place to rest and somewhere to sleep that evening.

He reached the edge of the plain and gazed down over a deep valley. Far in the distance he could just make out a distant village, smoke from the chimneys curling lazily into the evening sky.

He urged his horse down the switchback track to the valley floor. He was already anticipating an ice cold drink to quench his thirst, the taste of local delicacies, and good companionship.

When he reached the edge of the village it seemed deserted. There was just one street with houses and a few shops each side. But through the haze of evening he could barely distinguish some kind of activity at the far end of the community.

Urging his horse forward he realised all the villagers were gathered around a fence, which surrounded a field. As he drew closer he could hear the nervous shouts of the people. When they saw him they pleaded, "Help us, Señor. Save us from the monster."

The traveller looked into the field. All he could see was a huge watermelon.

"Please save us, Señor. It's going to attack."

"That's not a monster. It's a watermelon. It's just a rather oversized fruit."

"It's a monster, and it's going to attack. Help us."

"It's a watermelon."

"It's a monster."

"It's a water…"

But before he could finish the enraged villagers pulled him from his horse and threw him into the fishpond. Afterwards they lashed him to his horse and harried him out of the village.

An hour or so later another traveller was following hard on the heels of the former. The sun was already lower in the west, and he was feeling even thirstier and hungrier than the first traveller. He too contemplated a drink and good honest food of the region.

He snaked down the side of the valley and reached the outskirts of the village. He saw the crowd agitated and shouting by the fence.

"What's the problem?" he asked.

"Look, a fierce green monster. It's going to attack us."

"So there is," said the traveller. "It's big, and it's certainly fierce. Let me help you."

He drew his sword, spurred on his horse, leaped the fence, and in no time at all bits of watermelon were flying everywhere. The villagers, covered in red slush and black pips, were cheering and clapping. The traveller was carried in triumph through the village and invited to stay as long as he wished.

They put him in the best room at the hotel, they paid all his expenses, they served him the best food and the best wines of the region. And in return he took time to listen and learn about their culture, their history, their stories, their way of life.

And as he did so, little by little, he won the trust and confidence of these people. He began to tell them about his culture, his history, his stories, and the way of life of his own people. And very gently and delicately he began to teach them the difference between a monster and a watermelon.

And so in the fullness of time, the villagers began to plant and cultivate watermelons in their fields. And when the time finally came for the traveller to leave he passed by the field now full of rows and rows of massive watermelons awaiting harvest. And a villager said, "Thank you so much, Señor. You have taught us many things.

And you have shown us how to tame the watermelon and make it work for us."

And the traveller said, "You indeed have fine watermelons. But always remember, even watermelons can sometimes be monsters."

Primary source: Christina Hall.
Secondary sources: There are other versions in In Your Hands by Jane Revell & Susan Norman and NLP at Work by Sue Knight. See bibliography.

5.06   Walking to Learn

A colleague of mine from Rosario, Argentina, had been having problems with a student. Try as he might, the student seemed unable to learn. Yet he was intelligent, willing, and motivated.

Claudia was the director of a private language school. She had been running this particular class for a couple of months, and Jorge had achieved consistently poor results. Both Claudia and Jorge were equally frustrated. No matter how hard he tried Jorge was unable to rise from his lowly status as the weakest member of the class in written tests.

Claudia was puzzled. She knew that Jorge was driven to succeed in his career. At the age of twenty he held a promising position in an Argentinian engineering company that had sister companies elsewhere in Latin America and in Europe. Jorge desperately wanted to travel in his work for the company, and for that he needed to master English. He wanted to succeed but something seemed to be holding him back.

Claudia took him aside one day. "What stops you learning?"

"I don't know," he replied. "I try really hard but it just doesn't seem to go in."

Claudia tried a different tack. "Are you studying anything else?"

"Sure. I have lots of exams to pass in engineering. I'm studying all the time."

"How are you doing?"

"Fine," said Jorge. "No problem. Top scores."

Claudia was curious about this anomaly. She asked, "Where do you study for your engineering exams?"

"At home."

"Tell me about it. How do you study? What exactly do you do?"

"Well, I have my own room, and there's a big desk along one wall. I put all my books and papers that I have to study in front of me on the desk. Open, all the way along in a way that pleases me. Then I put some of my favourite music CDs in the music centre and as they play I kind of dance to the music, moving around the chair and along the desk in time to the music, reading whatever I think is important to read next. And it just goes in, the information I need just goes in without any real effort. Easy."

Claudia thought for a moment. Then she asked, "Jorge, can you play your favourite music silently inside your own head?"

He thought for a moment and then replied, "Sure, anyone can do that I guess."

"OK," said Claudia. "Let's try an experiment. You sit at a desk at the back of the class. During the lesson you can play the music you like inside your head. You can move around, in time with the music, as much as you like *provided* you don't disturb anyone else. And let's see if that makes any difference. If it works for you at home, maybe it might just work here at school. Want to try?"

Jorge looked excited, a smile spread across his face, and his feet began to tap.

Four weeks later his work had improved to such an extent that his test scores placed him tenth in that class of twenty. In another four weeks he scored top marks, and after that his performance got better and better.

"He was," as Claudia told me later, "a student who absolutely needed to move in order to learn. Whether he sat down in my class because he thought that's what he should do or because he thought I expected it of him, I don't know. What we both know now is that sitting down to learn was inhibiting him severely.

"What he learned is how to accelerate his learning to get more of what he wants. He now works in Paris. What I learned is that to get the best out of my students I need to help them each discover how they learn best, and make my teaching and classroom

149

management flexible enough to accommodate the learning needs each one of them has.

"Jorge taught me a powerful lesson. That if a learner can't learn in the way a teacher teaches, the teacher needs to learn to teach in the way the learners learn."

Primary source: Patricia Latorre.

5.07 A Silver Thread of Insight

In the early 1980s I contracted malaria while working in Tanzania. Lying on my bed in a hotel situated on the lower slopes of Kilimanjaro, I alternated between bouts of icy coldness and fever-ish heat. I must have dozed off for the next time I "awoke" nothing was as it had ever been before in my life.

I was, or rather my mind or spirit or soul—call it what you will—was, hovering near the ceiling in a top corner of the room, and I found myself looking down on my own body. I could see myself clearly, lying asleep on sheets bathed in sweat. Curiously, there was no panic or concern. Only a sense of deep calm. I can also remember my amused but detached surprise at seeing myself con-nected to my body by a thin silver thread. And the amusement came because years before I had scoffed at an account of a similar experience in one of Shirley MacLaine's books.

I don't remember the process of reconnection, and I certainly had no tools or framework through which I could understand the process of what had happened to me. For years I used to make fun of the story and of myself. It was clearly an important event, but mystifying, unknowable, unexplainable.

I let the experience slowly recede into the depths of my memory for the next fifteen or so years, until one day in the mid 1990s I was a student on a personal development course. At the time I had a number of reservations about the methods and contents of the course. And of certain things I was downright sceptical. One par-ticular task we were asked to do was to walk back along a "time-line" in order to recover past forgotten experiences in a particular context. The context I wanted to work on was peacefulness and tranquillity. I had no recollection in my conscious memory of ever having been in such a state in my life.

With large portions of scepticism in mind, yet the openness at least to give it a try, I laid out my timeline on the floor in front of me. I set my future to the right and my past to the left. Given the space of the room I was in, my birth date was about four metres to my left. At the age of 45 I stepped onto my NOW. And began to walk slowly backwards into my past.

Nothing happened as I stepped back, pace by pace, into my own history. And then suddenly a third of the way or so down the line I couldn't move. It was as if a hundred gentle hands were holding me in check. And instantly I knew what the experience was. It was the memory of malaria, my time on the ceiling, and I was flooded almost immediately with the same profound feeling of peacefulness and calm.

My colleague who was taking me through the exercise, a much more experienced practitioner than I, asked me to step off the line to a place where I could look on the experience with more detachment. He asked me what the experience had been, for he had noticed the sudden shift in my physiology as I connected with the power of the memory.

I told him about the experience. With great sensitivity he asked if I had been scared.

"No, not at all," I said, "it was just incredibly peaceful." I told him I had never known such calm in my life, before or since.

"Why weren't you scared?" he asked gently.

"Because I knew I'd go back."

And then he asked a simple but brilliant question, a question that changed my life. He said, "How did you know that?"

And without a flash of hesitation the answer came, so quick and so sure that it did not have time to be consciously framed. It was as if the answer had been waiting years for me to finally recognise it. I said, "Because I've got things to do."

It was the first time in my life that I had ever really connected with the idea that I am here on earth for a purpose and that I have a mission to fulfil. I wasn't sure then exactly what it was but the new direction that it set me in has made all the difference. And of course it raised the question of what other significant events in my life contain important and powerful messages that still await my attention and interpretation? What else have I missed through living too much on the surface? Through being too incurious?

5.08   Behavioural Flexibility

An armada of the US Navy was engaged in naval exercises off the coast of Canada when the following radio exchange was recorded:

#1:   "Please divert your course 15 degrees to the north to avoid danger of collision."

#2:   "Recommend that you divert *your* course 15 degrees to the south to avoid danger of a collision."

#1:   "We repeat. Divert north now to avoid collision."

#2:   "Strongly recommend you divert south soonest to avoid mishap."

#1:   "This is the Captain of a US Navy warship. I say again, divert your course with immediate effect."

#2:   "Copy. We say divert south now."

#1:   *"This is the USS Enterprise. We are an aircraft carrier of the US Navy. Divert your course NOW!"*

#2:   "We are a Canadian lighthouse. Your call!"

Primary source: The Daily Telegraph.

5.09   That Won't Work

It was a four-day course in Vienna at one of the Pedagogical Institutes. There were about thirty teachers, trainers, and educators attending the course. The topic was cooperative learning, team dynamics in business-speak. At the regular evaluation sessions everybody reported satisfaction with the way the programme was going. They enjoyed the activities, they liked the process of working in groups, of having to share information with each other in order to complete tasks. They were learning and having fun. Everybody thought they could use the ideas, the processes, and the activities with their students.

Except Werner Bichlmeyer.

His was the lone voice of dissent. His reasons were many and various. They concerned mainly two areas. First, the amount of additional preparation he would have to do. He had been teaching for twenty-five years, had all his lessons prepared, and valued the time he spent on his hobbies and various sports. His second area of concern was his views about his students. He felt them unable to take on board the responsibilities required by group work and cooperative engagement. He thought they might take advantage of group situations and do less work. He thought they might behave in childish ways and there would be an increase in what he perceived as indiscipline. He felt students would not want to share information and ideas, and above all that he might lose control.

These responses of Werner's leaked out slowly, evaluation session by evaluation session. After a while the group began to respond to him as a stuck record. He was certainly stubborn in, and committed to, his views. I did my best to win him around, to reframe his views, to challenge him to see things from other perspectives, to listen to the views of his colleagues, and the examples of success given by those educators already using these techniques.

Without success.

And I admired him for sticking to his guns in the face of such overwhelming opposition. He could easily have pretended it might work for him and avoided the censure of his peers. At the end I said, "Werner, I've tried everything I know to get you to see it differently. And I have to admit I've failed spectacularly."

"Yes," he said. "It won't work."

"Werner," I replied, "while that remains your belief, I have no doubt you are absolutely right. And you have every right to hold that belief, and I wish you well with your teaching. There are many ways to teach, and there is no right way. Just different ways that suit different kinds of learners. We make our choices, and I wish you the very best of luck."

A year later I was back at the same institution to run another four-day programme on a different topic. As I walked up the stairs at the beginning of the first day, I passed the large notice board advertising forthcoming courses. My course was there as well as many others.

But one particular notice caught my eye. It was a two-day seminar on cooperative learning. And the facilitator was none other than a certain Werner Bichlmeyer. I was intrigued.

Werner's course was due to take place a couple of weeks later, so I never got to talk to him about it. But, curious, I started wondering about what had happened. When did he change his mind about cooperative learning? A week later? A month? Six months? He certainly had changed his mind. And how come it was Werner who was offering such a public course, with all the preparation and work that required, and not one of the other twenty-nine educators who had so consistently espoused the cause?

It is quite common that those who most resist have most to learn. And, at a deep level, know this. Unlearning previously acquired skills, and even integrating new ideas into existing knowledge, takes effort and energy, and a degree of humility. The conscious mind sees the sacrifices needed and the time required, and baulks at it. The unconscious mind thinks WOW! and bides its time, searching for and integrating possibilities.

Every skill we have ever learned is a pattern. It has a structure and a sequence. It is our ability to run thousands upon thousands of patterns in our lives, at the level of unconscious competence—doing without thinking—that allows us to survive in a world of amazing complexity. Without this ability survival would be barely possible.

The oldest part of the brain understands this. The "reptilian" brain frequently resists new learning because it wishes to protect the acquired patterns that have allowed each one of us to survive successfully since birth. But at a higher level, the mid-brain and the neo-cortex have different kinds of wisdom. They search for possibility: if learning this new skill gives me an increased chance of survival and success, I'm open to it. And so the brain becomes more receptive, and learning becomes possible and even welcome.

Certainly it seemed likely to me that sometime during the previous twelve months the different parts of Werner's brain may have had a similar kind of internal dialogue.

5.10 The Faithful Servant

Once upon a time, there was a powerful king who had a craving for avocados. He thought so much of these fruit that he even had a servant whose only role was to prepare them according to all the best recipes.

The king couldn't get enough avocados. He worshipped, adored, and praised them to anyone who would listen. He said to his servant, "This plant is surely the greatest of all fruits. It is magnificent. Look here at the deep green and purple hues of its skin, feel the rough honesty of its texture protecting its smooth inner promise, and as for the smell and taste, there is nothing under Heaven to compare with it."

The servant replied, "My Lord, you are most certainly right."

It was not long after this that the King fell violently ill. And the cause was none other than overindulgence in avocado eating. It was as if all the avocados he had ever eaten now wanted to revisit themselves upon him. His stomach was swollen and painful. Neither sitting nor standing were comfortable for him. He felt absolutely dreadful.

The King cursed the avocado. "Never let me see another avocado as long as I live. Remove every single one from my kitchens and royal gardens. Destroy every avocado in the kingdom. They are disgusting and evil, the fruits of the Devil Herself. Just the thought of one makes me feel ill."

The servant replied, "My Lord, you are most certainly right."

The King stopped in his tracks, paused a while, and then looked sternly at the servant. "Wait a moment," he said. "Just the other day you agreed with me that the avocado was the best among all fruits. Now that I have changed my opinion, I find that you too have done the same. How do you explain this?"

"My Lord, that's easy to answer. I am your servant, not the avocado's."

Primary source: Nossrat Peseschkian.
General source: Oriental tradition.

5.11 *Michelangelo*

Under a hot sun, a little boy is gazing at a young man intently chipping away at a large piece of rock.

"Why are you doing that?"

"Because," said Michelangelo, "there's an angel inside, and he wants to come out."

Primary source: Anecdotal.

5.12   *The Happiest Man in the World*

A man who had every material comfort, money, and possessions, nevertheless felt that something significant was missing in his life. He felt a yearning and inner emptiness. So he went to someone reputed to be a fine healer.

The Healer said, "This is a normal and everyday malady for many people who have more than they need. If you wish to be cured it is not a difficult thing, but it will take patience and some courage. Are you ready for the challenge?"

The man said he was ready.

"Then your task is simple. All you need to do is find the happiest man in the world and wear his shirt. Once you have his shirt you will attain the peace you seek."

So the man set off in search of the happiest man in the world. His search took him to all corners of the world. He found many happy men, and women too. He heard great amounts of laughter and saw copious smiles, but every happy person he found always said there was one happier than she or he was.

Finally the man found a mountain, on which many agreed the world's happiest man lived. From far away he heard peals of laughter rolling down the mountain and across the valleys. The man was so happy that even the flowers were smiling and the trees were singing.

"Are you the happiest man in the world?" asked the pilgrim.

"Indeed I am. There is none happier than I anywhere in the world," said the happiest man between gales of laughter.

"Then, so that I may find peace and tranquillity in my life at last, may I respectfully make a request?"

"Go ahead, my friend."

"Would you be so good as to give me your shirt? I will reward you handsomely for it."

The happiest man in the world howled with glee. His laughter seemed uncontrollable. So much so that the traveller was rather affronted.

"I don't see what's so funny about my request."

"Well," said the happiest man, "if you had any powers of observation you would have noticed that I'm not wearing a shirt. In fact, I don't possess a single one."

"Then what am I to do? My Healer, who is one of the most respected in the world, said that this was the only way I could be cured from my yearning."

"Then you will indeed be cured. For it is the desire to seek for something that may be unattainable that marks out the achiever from the non-achiever. For the higher you set your expectations of yourself the more you will approach your full potential."

And saying this the happiest man in the world removed the cap from his head and it turned out to be none other than the healer himself.

The man was somewhat confused, disappointed, and even a little angry about this. "Why didn't you tell me this when I first came to see you?"

"Because you had to reconnect with real experience in the world. You were not then ready to understand these things. You had to submit to the experience of life in all its ways and forms in order to understand that happiness and suffering are interconnected sides of the same coin."

Primary source: Idries Shah.
General source: Sufi tradition.

5.13   *The Shirt of a Happy Man*

A rich Sultan lay dying. He lay on his bed on gorgeous silk sheets, propped up on splendid and richly ornamented silk pillows. All around him the wealth of the Sultan was evident in every artefact and in the number of eminent doctors who were attending him.

The doctors agreed this was a hopeless case, but there was one slim possibility. If the shirt of a happy man could be found and placed beneath the Sultan's head, then perhaps there would be a chance.

Messengers, soldiers, police, and even released convicts were despatched to the four corners of the kingdom to find a happy man. Everywhere they looked they found misery and despondency. In the cities, in the towns, in the villages it was the same story. The people had nothing to share but trouble and care.

Eventually, when all hope seemed to be gone, some of the searchers met a shepherd who had been spending the summer in a high and remote valley. He smiled and laughed, sang and whistled. When asked he said, "Am I happy? I can't imagine anyone who could be more happy than me."

"Then please give us your shirt," they said, "for we need it to save the life of the Sultan."

"I wish I could help, but I don't possess a shirt," replied the shepherd. "Never have."

When this news was given to the Sultan he dismissed everybody from his bedroom and considered the information deeply for seven days.

At the end of his contemplation he made a decision, and ordered that all his silks and artefacts, the contents of his vast treasure chests should be distributed amongst the people.

Legend says that from this moment the Sultan began to recover his health. And his happiness.

Primary source: Nossrat Peseschkian.
General source: Oriental tradition.

5.14   *Picasso*

Picasso was on the point of becoming famous. He was travelling first class from Nice to Paris. Sharing his compartment was a wealthy American art collector.

The American thought he recognised the artist. "Hey, aren't you Mr Pablo Picasso?"

"Si," said Picasso.

"Listen," said the collector, "Why don't you paint people as they really are?"

"¿Que?" said Picasso.

"Why don't you paint people as they really are? I mean, if I look at one of your paintings it just ain't real. You got an eye in the middle of the forehead, a nose where an ear should be. It's just ridiculous. It's all wrong. It's not real and it's not art!"

"I don't know what you mean," said the artist.

"Art should reflect life. Hold a mirror up to nature and all that. You gotta paint people as they really are."

"I still don't understand," said Picasso.

"OK wise guy, I'll show you what I mean." The American took his wallet from his jacket, opened it, and took out a photograph.

"Look," said the American. "This is my wife, that's how she really is."

"Oh, now I understand," Picasso said in a serious manner. "Your wife is extremely thin and about 10 centimetres tall."

Primary source: Anecdotal.
Secondary source: There is a version in Joseph O'Connor & John Seymour, Introducing NLP. See bibliography.

5.15   Acorns

A young traveller, backpacking
Dry remote barren uplands
Lost
Old shepherd, invitation
Counting acorns into rows
Traveller curious; shepherd reticent
Morning: shepherd in distance: bending?

50 years later, traveller returns
Wants to revisit
Cartography problem
No barren uplands
Only oak forests and tumbling streams
Puzzled

In the early summer of 1914, a young Italian student was hiking in the Pyrenees Mountains. He was in a particularly remote and barren area that nevertheless had a rugged and savage beauty. In the particular upland valley that he had entered, there was no vegetation except coarse mountain grass and the occasional stunted and wind-gnarled tree. In this high wilderness he felt free from so many pressures he had left behind at home. Here he found a useful and suitably distant perspective from which to view the world.

He was an experienced mountain walker with excellent natural navigation and map reading skills. It was not uncommon for him to spend days alone in the mountains. He felt at home here. But on this particular day in the Pyrenees as he watched the sun slowly descending towards the mountain summits in the west, he experienced a frisson of foreboding.

He realised he was lost. And he knew that meant danger. For here there was neither shelter nor water, and his meagre supplies of food were almost exhausted. If only he could find a village—but he had no idea where the nearest village was.

He continued to follow the sun, all the time scanning the horizon for signs of civilisation or habitation. Just before the sun met the distant mountain peaks, he thought he could discern movement far off. He picked up his pace and soon he could not only see the woolly forms of dirty sheep, but hear their bells and bleats too. Not long after, he was able to pick out the dark shadowy form of their weather-beaten shepherd sitting motionless beneath an overhanging rock.

The old shepherd invited the young man to spend the night with him in his simple hut, saying it was too far and too late to reach the nearest village. They sat together in silence around a small fire, sharing the old man's dinner of sheep's cheese, bread, and good local wine.

The shepherd was a man of few words. It was hard for the student to gather much information about anything, except for directions to the nearest village, and this the old man showed mostly with the aid of a stick, drawing a map in the dusty earth.

After the meal, the shepherd stood up and disappeared into the hut, emerging moments later with an old coffee sack. Without a word he emptied the contents on the ground next to the fire. There were hundreds of acorns. The shepherd sat down, and after carefully scrutinising each acorn he put some in a general pile, and some in lines.

After half an hour of concentration, the shepherd seemed satisfied with his evening's work. He had in front of him ten rows of acorns, with exactly ten acorns in each row. And a large general pile to his left. He then proceeded to put each row of ten acorns in ten separate pockets of his large shepherd's coat, and the rest of the acorns he put back in the sack, which he then returned to its hook inside the hut.

With a simple nod of his head and a rough handshake he indicated that it was bedtime. It was the last the Italian saw of the shepherd. Next morning, when the student awoke to another brilliant day, the shepherd had long since left. Scanning the horizon, he thought he could perhaps see distant woolly movement, but in the shimmer of the heat he couldn't be sure. And he thought too, that perhaps he could also make out a dark shapeless form bending down and, with a stick, pushing hard and rhythmically into the barren earth.

The young hiker reached the village safely, enjoyed the rest of his walking holiday, and returned home. It was soon to be a turbulent period, but through all the many following years, the Italian never totally forgot that experience. The barrenness and remoteness of that high valley, its absence of water and habitation, the old shepherd and his acorns.

It was a memory that stayed. It would go and then return. And he began to be curious to see that valley again.

It took him fifty years.

So, one Roman summer, the ageing hiker in his Campervan, with his wife, and those of his children and grandchildren who cared to accompany him, set out for the borders between France and Spain, to the remote and barren valley which the old hiker had so often fondly referred to.

And they watched out expectantly for the barren dryness, the remote inaccessibility, and the vast open spaces of mountain grass and wind-gnarled trees.

But they saw none of these things. The old hiker thought the maps must be wrong, for he knew he had lost none of his map reading skills. He just couldn't understand it. He became more and more puzzled. For where there should have been a wide, remote, and barren valley now they could only find tumbling streams, small but thriving villages cultivating vegetables and flowers, and above all row upon row, acre upon acre, of sturdy, mature oak trees shimmering in the sunlight.

"Oh no! That just can't be possible," he thought.

Primary source: Brigitte Woehrer.
Secondary source: Jean Giono, The Man Who Planted Trees, Harvill Press.

Section 6

Transition

Transition

"Why is this section so short?"

"Either for mathematical reasons, or because the writer doesn't like long goodbyes," the Magician replied.

"Or maybe both," the Young Apprentice added.

6.01 An Irish Blessing

May the road rise to meet you.
May the wind be always at your back.
May the sun shine warm upon your face.
And may the rains fall soft upon your fields.

Walk in peace and contentment
Wherever on your road you may be,
And till we meet again
May God hold you gently in the hollow of His hand.

Primary source: Carmita Galvao.
Secondary source: Anthony Robbins, Unlimited Power. See bibliography.

6.02   *Five Silver Stars*

Five silver stars fell from the sky.

The first is for me for writing these stories down.

The second is for you for reading them.

The third is for all the storytellers from whom I learned these stories.

And the fourth is for all the storytellers who told my storytellers their stories, an ancestry stretching far back into the mists of time.

The fifth is for all of you who pass on, in your own way, these stories to someone else. When you pass on a story, giving it your stamp, you add to the sum of knowledge in the world, and you confirm your own immortal creativity.

Primary source: Hugh Lupton, '3 Golden Apples'.

Some Ways to Use the Metaphors and Stories in this Book

"I understand why story and metaphor can be useful, important, and even at times essential to the excellent communicator," said the Young Apprentice. "They can demonstrate the relevance of taking a certain action, or thinking about things in a different way, and they can build influential relationships between the storyteller and the listeners, or change the mood and energy in a room, and many other things beside. There is a lot of information about all this in the Introduction to the book.

"I also understand what metaphor is and how it operates through language, and the impact it has on the mind. There is also information in the bibliography that will lead me into further exploration of these things through the books written by Wizards.

"I also know much more about how to become a more effective storyteller as a result of the tips given in the Introduction and the usefulness of asking for and listening to feedback. I know that feedback is 'The Breakfast of Champions', as it says in the story called 'Three Steps To Success' [1.08].

"But what I'm not so sure about yet is how and where I can apply stories and metaphors. How do I know when it would be a good idea to offer these to a person or a group? In what circumstances do they work best, and which story should I choose? Should I always use stories for a purpose or is it alright just to use them for entertainment?"

The Master was thoughtful for a moment. "Entertainment is, in my view, one of the higher purposes of life. It is quite possible to be totally serious in intention about an issue and still be entertaining. But your questions about applications are excellent ones. So let us address the issue of where, when, and how to apply metaphors to the processes of affirmation, challenge, and transformation."

The Elusiveness of Precision, the Power of Ambiguity

"There are many ways of using the stories in this book," the Magician said, "as many as there are thoughts that can generate them. Any ideas I can offer you right now will necessarily be limited by my own lived experience. Tomorrow, which is a metaphor in itself, I may have more ideas, but for now what follows will have to do. Your own experience, brought to bear on these stories, will add richness to the infinite amount of interpretations possible. And that is also true of anyone who reads this book when they apply themselves to looking below the surface of the narrative, below the surface of life!

"In the introduction the writer talked about the art of *framing*. Framing sets the story within a particular context. Without a frame the story can mean whatever the listener-reader chooses it to mean on the basis of his or her own experiences or current obsessions. With a frame the storyteller has much more influence over how a story is understood and interpreted. Yet even so there will always be plenty of scope for differences of opinion and interpretation. It is not an exact science!"

"So stories are ambiguous and vague," stated the Little Apprentice.

"Without a frame that is indeed the case. The storyteller has no power or management over how they may be understood. But at times, depending on the purpose of the storyteller, that will be an excellent strategy.

"Sometimes, the very vagueness of the metaphor allows the listener-reader to do the very inner work they most need. If you want to know more about the power of artfully vague language and its power to heal, I suggest you read the works of the Wizard Milton Erickson, some of whose work you will find in the bibliography.

So for now let us deal with the uses of vagueness first and uses of framing later.

"It is not just story and metaphor that are ambiguous," the Master continued. "Ambiguity is at the very heart of language. After all, language is a representation of something, not the thing itself. You do not eat the menu in a restaurant, the words don't taste the same as the food. Except of course in some fast food chains where the menu possibly tastes better than the food itself."

The Apprentice looked a bit puzzled by this until he realised from the expression on the Magician's face that it was supposed to be a joke.

"Let me give you an illustration of the ambiguity of language," the Magician continued. "Many years ago when I was attending a Wizards' Conference in Hong Kong, a fellow Wizard invited another to accompany him for a walk on one of the many beautiful and rugged outlying islands. They arranged a meeting point at the ferry pier on the island and met at the appointed time.

"My colleague arrived dressed in T-shirt, old cotton trousers, and a pair of walking boots." The Apprentice seemed a little shocked at the idea of a Magician dressed so casually, but the Master continued. "He also carried their picnic in a strong plastic bag. She arrived in a beautifully embroidered silk dress wearing high-heeled shoes. Their idea of a walk was not the same. Whereas his expectation was a demanding hike over rough terrain and a picnic on a remote hillside overlooking the blue expanses of the South China Sea, hers was a gentle stroll along the promenade ending some 300 metres later in one of the excellent air-conditioned seafood restaurants on the quayside."

The Young Apprentice thought it would be a good idea to have the picnic *and* the seafood.

"This sort of miscommunication," continued the Master, "which seems endemic even to speakers of the same language, suggests that interpretation can be infinite. Was the vaguely interpreted 'walk' an example of comedy or tragedy, or something in between? Or was it both, depending on whether you were one of

177

those involved or an impartial observer? Did both of those involved feel the same way about the situation and its consequences? Was it just another amusing anecdote or were somebody's hopes and dreams of some kind of imagined future altered forever?"

"So what *does* a story mean?" asked the Apprentice, impatient to get to the point.

"Let me give you an example. An Italian Wizard recently sent me the following story that she had downloaded from the internet. The story is followed by interpretations from listeners and readers. What I found particularly fascinating was that the interpretations appear to say just as much about the interpreters as they do about the story itself."

Self-Control

One day there was an earthquake that shook the entire Zen temple. Parts of it even collapsed. Many of the monks were terrified. When the earthquake stopped the teacher said, "Now you have had the opportunity to see how a Zen man behaves in a crisis situation. You may have noticed that I did not panic. I was quite aware of what was happening and what to do. I led you all to the kitchen, the strongest part of the temple. It was a good decision, because you see we have all survived without any injuries. However, despite my self-control and composure, I did feel a little bit tense, which you may have deduced from the fact that I drank a large glass of water, something I never do under ordinary circumstances."

One of the monks smiled, but didn't say anything.

"What are you laughing at?" asked the teacher.

"That wasn't water," the monk replied, "it was a large glass of soy sauce."

People's reactions to this story:

"I see this sort of behaviour often in men. They feel they have to put on a front to appear to be something that they are not."

"It's like someone bragging about how cool they are, and then you find out that he is just a geek underneath after all."

"Sounds just like my father—always in control, always right, always the leader. But WE know the truth!"

"Sometimes the calmest-looking person in an emergency situation is really the most nervous."

"Someone should have thrown that water into that teacher's face so he could wake up and realize that he was kidding himself."

"This reminds me of people who think they are so great and are always bragging about it. Admitting that they are wrong is the hardest thing in their lives, when it should be something that's very natural."

"Everyone at one time or another has been in a tense situation where you think that you are composed and in control, but then you do something weird—which shows that you're not."

"Sometimes, when you're in a very stressful situation, you aren't aware of your actions until someone else points them out."

"It didn't matter to him what he drank. He wasn't concentrating on the taste, but instead on the action."

"Even a Zen man is still human."

"I'd tell this story to children so they wouldn't be afraid to be afraid."

"How can you be so shaken that you can't tell the difference between water and soy sauce?!"

"I think the teacher was testing the monks—to see if they noticed what he drank."

"I think the teacher deliberately was trying to teach them that it's OK to do something weird in a panic situation. You can do something weird, but for the important decisions you still can make the right choices."

"Maybe the soy sauce explains why he is so relaxed."

"I really thought this story was going to have a great ending, but it was stupid."

Primary source: Mara Pedretti.
Secondary source: Zen Stories to Tell Your Neighbours Website (John Suler PhD).

"Hey!" said the Young Apprentice. "It's unbelievable just how different people are."

"So what have you learned from this?" said the Master.

There was a pause for reflection, and then the Apprentice took a deep breath and began. "The ambiguity of metaphor is precisely what makes it so exciting. Without a frame, stories can mean whatever the reader or listener decides they mean. So they allow the listener-reader to select the meaning or meanings that best relate to, and resonate with, their own inner maps of reality."

"Exactly! An unframed metaphor allows the reader-listener to do their own inner work, comparing the behaviours and attitudes revealed within the story to their own behaviours and attitudes. Sometimes a story will affirm a reader's model of the world, and sometimes it will contradict and challenge it. Learning, and action upon learning, will depend on the inner state of the interpreter, whether he or she is open, arrested, or closed to change. And that will also be information for the storyteller.

"Unframed stories leave interpretation open to chance. On the other hand, if a communicator knows the other person well, he or she will be able to predict the probable response of the listener-reader to the story. This is a particularly useful application for a parent, a teacher, a health worker, or a therapist. Although the storyteller leaves the metaphor unframed, the receiver provides their own frame as a result of their present preoccupation or the current situation."

Framing: An Overview

"So when and why would you put a frame around a story?" asked the Apprentice with curiosity. "And how do you do it?"

"Let me take those questions one at a time. While many people will read the stories in this book simply for pleasure, out of curiosity, and quite randomly, others will have different motives, outcomes, and intentions. These people are likely to be communicators in a wide variety of communication and relationship contexts. They will be primarily people working in the areas of personal and professional development."

"Such as?"

"Such as teachers, trainers, facilitators, presenters, coaches, counsellors, mentors, managers, leaders, health workers, and therapists. And they may also be parents, partners, and friends. They could even be politicians or lawyers. These people will often wish to put a *frame* around a story in order to 'shape' or direct its meaning. They will need to draw the attention of their listeners to a particular way of understanding the significance of the story within a specific context. In this way the listener is encouraged to make the connections desired by the communicator and move towards a new understanding or perspective."

"But isn't that manipulation?" demanded the Apprentice, shocked.

"A very good question. Handled inappropriately it could of course be manipulation. Handled elegantly and, above all, ethically it is what we call influence."

"What's the difference?" The Apprentice was sceptical and showing encouraging signs of independent thinking.

"You are right in understanding that there is a fine line between manipulation and influence. So let me offer you a definition of the difference. Imagine, if you will, manipulation sitting here on my left hand. Manipulation means I know what I want and I'm determined to get it. If you get in the way, too bad. I'll get what I want in spite of you.

"Here on my right hand is influence. Influence means I know what I want and I'm determined to get it. However, influence understands the world as a system, and communication as a systemic loop involving two or more players. Influence says I know what I want, and to get it I'll need to find out what you want too. Let us then discover and put together our shared needs and outcomes and work co-intentionally to get what we both want."

"But that could take ages."

"Sometimes, but usually it's quite possible to achieve successful results for both parties quickly. This is often true even between parties that are quite antagonistic to each other. The art is called influencing with integrity. I may have to do a little bit of negotiating, but the great advantage is that I have now built a relationship of mutual trust and respect that will last over time. Next time I want to achieve something which involves the same people I am likely to have influence with them rather than resistance. Personally I'd rather have allies at the gates of the pass than enemies. If you want to read more about this I recommend you read the book written by the Genie Laborde. You'll find it in the bibliography."

"Isn't she a Wizard?"

"Genies are also Wizards."

"So am I right in thinking," pressed the Apprentice, "that when you put a frame around a story it is as much because of your concern for the needs and welfare of the other people as it is for yourself?"

"Precisely," replied the Master, "and that is why you must apply metaphor with a clear outcome in mind, using integrity, appropriacy, and respect, and having taken time to discover as much as you need to know about the needs of the others.

"So tell me, what have you understood from our discussion so far?"

The Apprentice drew a breath, paused and began. "The art of framing allows the communicator—the storyteller—to direct the listeners' attention towards a particular channel or direction. The possibilities of interpretation may be closed down quite rigorously or left artfully vague and ambiguous. Whether the choice is precise direction or artful vagueness, or something in between, will depend on the intentions of the storyteller, the results he or she wishes to achieve—with respect and integrity—through the application of metaphor."

"Very good. However, the choice of frame is not always in the hands of the communicator. Sometimes the frame is provided by an event that happens or arises unexpectedly during the course of an interaction. Somebody asks a challenging question, a student says 'I don't want to do this', a delegate breaks down in tears or questions the authority of the workshop leader, or a team member attempts to sabotage or undermine a project. The communicator in this case can respond with a story that addresses the frame created by the unexpected intervention."

"Now, that's exactly what I want to know more about," said the Apprentice enthusiastically. "How do I know what stories to use when and where?"

The Art of Framing: Its Various Purposes and Applications

To the Apprentice's questions the Magician replied, "I am reluctant to be exhaustive on this issue. Partly because I wish to leave space for others to do their own exploration, and partly because, like everyone else, I am bound for now within my own present limitations. However, let me take a small number of stories from within this book and look at a number of different ways and frames in which they could be used."

"Great," said the Apprentice. "Besides, when some of my teachers pretend they know all the answers I get very irritated. Where's my space to do my own thinking?"

"Quite right," said the Master. "I'll say as little as I need and then shut up. Tell me if I go on too long. Do we have a deal?"

The Apprentice smiled and shook the Master's proffered hand.

The Jar [Section 1.03]

"Let's start with the story 'The Jar'. It's a story from an old tradition, and you can find many variations of it. It has many possible meanings and applications, and of course you could let readers and listeners explore these variations for themselves and share them together. That's a great way to let them understand just how different they can be from each other and in their understandings of their experience and of language itself.

"But I often use this story at the beginning of certain courses I run, and I use this story for a number of specific yet different reasons."

"Such as what?" said the Apprentice, paying great attention.

"For me this story is like an overture at the opera. At the opera the overture introduces tunes and themes that will be expanded and developed as the story progresses. And I use this story in the same way to flag up issues and themes the delegates and I will investigate and explore during the course of the training programme."

"Why is it important to do that?" asked the Apprentice.

"First, it teases and attracts the participants. Would you go fishing and fail to put something interesting for the fish on the hook at the end of your line? Every communication needs some kind of introduction and suggestion of relevance and purpose that motivates the listeners to pay attention.

"Second, the human brain is less likely to resist something it has already heard about and experienced, no matter how briefly.

"Third, a story told at the beginning of a course or presentation is unusual and often unexpected. It attracts attention, alters and engages with the emotional states of the participants. Some may become curious, fascinated, and excited. Others may be irritated or frustrated. No matter! I have got their attention and shifted their attention from what they were thinking about previously to what I am communicating with them now."

"I see. It's like the way some movies start with an exciting action moment to get attention, and then go backwards in time to trace the past events that lead up to it."

"A useful analogy and a strategy that could well be used."

"So what are the lessons you want to draw our attention to in this story?"

"Well, here are some of them." The Master turned to a flipchart and began to write:

Possible frames: *A course on the principles of communication*
                        A course on practical presentation skills
                        A course on building influential relationships

Key inferences:
- We each experience and interpret the world differently

- The meaning of our message is the response we get

- Everybody's view has a right to be heard and respected within a group regardless of perceived status

- This is a learning environment

- There is always more to learn

- Learning in this environment will sometimes be conducted through metaphor

- It is a good idea to build on sound foundations before you attempt more sophisticated skills

- Learning and its application require structuring and patterning; organise your thinking into hierarchies and store information as generalisations rather than details

- The professor has wisdom but his wisdom is limited

- The learners have wisdom and their contributions must be respected and acknowledged

- We take in information through our senses: in this case through internally visualising and externally reading non-verbal communication (visual); through listening to and interpreting words and tonality (auditory); and we also take in and process information through our emotional involvement (kinaesthetic).

- What are your rocks? In other words, what do you specifically want to get from this course?

"There are other possibilities too, but I don't want to deny your space. However, there is one thing more that I might well do in order to really connect with the group."

"What would that be?"

"Just after the beginning, near the start of the story, I might just add a couple of sentences. For example, 'The professor was sitting on an upright chair with a steel frame and a wooden seat and wooden back ... rather like the one I'm sitting on now. And the group were sitting around him in a semi-circle on chairs that were exactly the same ... rather like you are now.' By describing the chairs that you and the group are actually sitting on as being the same as those of the professor and his group you merge the reality of the story and the reality of the present group, creating an amusing yet slightly disturbing and provocative response. Anything is now possible."

The Art of Storytelling

The Apprentice was reflective for a while. The implications of disturbing and provoking a group seemed to connect with certain inner confusions and doubts of his own. "Is it important how well you tell the story?" asked the Apprentice.

"Of course it makes a difference. But don't expect to be perfect; there's no such thing as a perfect storyteller. Be yourself, make sure you know the structure of the story by practising it in advance, but develop the flexibility to tell the story slightly differently each time so it seems improvisational and alive. Give your story as a gift to the listeners so you can all enjoy it together."

"But I'll never be as good at telling stories as you."

"Do you think I was born telling stories?" The Magician shifted her vocal pitch to a slightly sterner tonality. "I've had to work very hard at it. Why? Because I believe that story telling's an essential tool in my communication toolkit, a powerful choice available to me to use when appropriate. I suggest you re-read the section on story telling techniques in the introduction. It will help you develop your skills and then you will learn as I did, by doing, making mistakes, and being open to feedback.

"And remember the first rule of personal and professional development. Always learn from an expert but never compare yourself with an expert. The only useful question to ask that will motivate you constantly to achieve more is this. How can I be more skilful today than I was yesterday? How can I ensure I am more skilful tomorrow than I am today? You are your best and most reliable measurement."

But the Apprentice was still not completely convinced. "But how do I do all that? I've *never* been able to tell a good story. I'll *never* be as good as you."

"Well, now that you have provided a frame that here we could usefully label 'abject pathetic-ness'"—the Master shifted to a more gentle tone accompanied by an amused smile—"you give me two choices. Either I could be direct and give you two straightforward instructions: practise and get feedback. Or I could offer you a metaphor in which the desired behaviour is modelled by the characters in the story. Which would you prefer?"

The Master began tickling the Apprentice who immediately forgot to be sulky and pathetic. After a while, and plenty of screaming and giggling, he pleaded for the Magician to stop. "No more please. I give in. Pleeeaaase! I'll take the story."

Once the Apprentice had composed himself, the Magician began.

"One of the great things about metaphor is that it focuses not on the problem, but on the solution to the problem. Take this manuscript of stories, read them this evening, choose one or two that are appropriate for your situation of being less than resourceful about story telling, and tell me tomorrow morning why you have chosen them. In other words, what possible applications can you find in these stories for your present lack of confidence? What lessons can you learn to effect useful change in yourself?"

Next morning, the Apprentice greeted the Magician, turned and wrote on the flipchart:

Three Steps to Success [1.08]

Frame: *A limiting belief that a person (in this case me) does not have access to the resources they need to make a desired change*

Key inferences:
- Success requires discipline and effort

- You need to know what you want in life and pursue it actively

- It is easy to get distracted

- Your greatest resources are yourself and other people

- Learn from the behaviour of successful people. See also Gandhi [1.05], Einstein [1.07], Edison [3.13], and Gary Player [3.14]

- Success does not happen by chance but through developing effective structures and patterns of behaviour that move a person from a present situation where one is not satisfied, to a desired situation where one has what one wants

- Change is possible and the solution to what I want lies within my gift and the action I take

You Have It or You Don't [4.02]

Frame: *The limiting belief that people are either born with a talent or without it and that nothing can be done about this situation*

Key inferences: Talent is based on dedication, practice, and intention
- Wisdom and talent are not always recognised

- Be true to yourself

- Theory is of no value without practice

- Power can be abused. Authority does not necessarily signify wisdom or intelligence

- Good leaders take advice

- Flexibility, and the ability to adapt to current conditions and make the best of them, is essential to a successful outcome

- Patience, under the right conditions, is a virtue. See also "Perceptual Positions" [1.15]

- Stories can teach us a lot. Knowledge is available in all cultures

"Excellent," said the Master. "You have found two stories that exactly suit the frame in which last night you found yourself. You have extracted key learnings that will be helpful to you, and to others too, when you share these stories."

"Master," said the Apprentice with excitement. "That's not all. This morning at breakfast some of my classmates were talking about the Wizarding exams we have to take at the end of this semester. Some were saying that they would never become successful Magicians, that they didn't have the talent or knowledge, and that it wasn't fair that some students found it so easy to learn. So guess what? I said, 'Think about what you've just been saying. Now wouldn't it be useful to stop all this negative thinking and instead look forward to the exams?' They looked surprised, I can tell you. But when I said, listen to these stories, they did. And it made them think; I could see that from their body language and the questions they asked afterwards.

"But the best thing was that I told the stories and they listened. I wasn't brilliant, and certainly not as good as you. But I did it, and now I know I can do it. And I also begin to understand how I can continue to get better at it. I'm on a journey."

"Yes," the Magician said. "You're on a journey, and you're not as good as me *yet!* So I too had better get thinking about the art of story telling so you don't catch me up. At least not for a while."

Using stories in presentations and other kinds of interaction

Beginnings, middles, and ends

"You've talked about starting an interaction with a story such as 'The Jar', but where else can I use stories in my presentations?"

"Anywhere," replied the Master. "You can plan in advance where to use them. For example, to open or close your presentation. Or you can use them at the beginning or end of a section within the presentation. You can also use them to illustrate a teaching point. In these cases you can insert them into your overall structure while you are planning your presentation.

"However, you can also use stories to respond to things that occur unexpectedly during the course of your presentation: a question perhaps, or when somebody asks you how they could apply this information in their own personal or professional life. This is what I did last night with you when you expressed your lack of confidence about story telling. Although in that case I asked you to find an appropriate story for yourself."

"What stories might you choose to begin and end a lesson or presentation?"

"I would always suggest that any story you use relates in some way to the topics and themes of your overall communication. It doesn't have to be clear straightaway. Your audience will work that out later. So, to answer your question, any story will do at the beginning provided it meets certain essential criteria.

"At the outset you need to do several crucial things with your audience whether one person or many:

- ✓ Get and maintain their attention

- ✓ Build a relationship with them that is appropriate to your outcome and theirs

- ✓ Enable them to perceive the relevance of what you will share with them

- ✓ Pitch your communication in a way that relates to their world, their reality, their way of being

- ✓ Use a story whose themes and ideas you will expand on during your presentation

Endings
"If you finish with a story, you need to keep certain other factors in mind. The ending of your communication, whether it is a lesson, a seminar, a presentation, a meeting, a sales event, an appraisal, a feedback session, a counselling session, or something

else, requires sensitive handling and an awareness of what you want to happen next.

"When you manage and run a communication event, whether it's a conversation or a presentation at a conference or something in between, it is absolutely essential that you have a clear goal in mind. What is the purpose of your presentation? If you don't know that, you are wasting everybody's time and showing disrespect. The end of your 'presentation' is your leverage point. This is where you hand over responsibility to your audience to take whatever action necessitated your presentation in the first place.

"People don't only take action rationally, as a thinking process, but also emotionally. During your interaction you will of course appeal to their logical reasoning abilities with a structured, clear, and well-organised argument. But you must also appeal to their emotional state. For this is what will send them away with the appropriate energy to take the actions you require from them."

"I'm not sure I understand," the Apprentice countered.

"Did your mother or father ever tell you stories at bedtime?"

"Of course."

"And how did the stories finish?"

"Mmmh. That's a good question. I often fell asleep before the end."

"What do you think was the purpose your parents had for telling you bedtime stories?"

There was a pause. "Well, of all the scheming, low-down tricks. They *wanted* me to fall asleep!" The Apprentice was rather shocked at this revelation.

"So what strategies did they use to enable that to happen?"

"OK, now I'm beginning to get the point. So what did they do? Hmmh! They would slow the story down, lower the tone of their voice, and use slow rhythmic patterns to induce in me the desire to sleep."

"Precisely, and you need to use appropriate patterns of words, tone, and energy to send your audience away in the most effective emotional state to take the action you want them to."

"For example," said the Apprentice warming to the theme, "if you want people to sell ideas you need to make them feel excited, confident, and passionate. But if you want people to be concerned about some serious issues at work you might use patterns that create emotional states such as reflection, introspection, and determination."

"Let me give you an example of a story I might use to end a seminar, especially if I want my audience to do some or all of the following things." The Magician turned to the flipchart and wrote:

- reflect on what they have learned

- take action on their learning

- read their training manuals

- search for meaning below the surface of things

- wonder at their untapped potential.

Pebbles [5.04]

Frame: *Ending of a seminar*
Purpose: *Summarise seminar*
         Indicate future choices for action and appropriate
         emotional state for putting action into practice

Key inferences:

- There is structure below the surface of things

- Assumptions can be limiting. See also the story "Assumptions" [4.12]

- You learn when you are ready to see the world as it is. See: "Not Yet Ready" [4.04] and "The Secret of Success" [3.02]

- The training manual contains jewels; life contains jewels. See: "Real Knowledge" [2.02]

- Maximising your potential requires you to be proactive, search out meanings, and take action

- We limit ourselves through our lack of awareness

- You will continue to learn, and in doing so you will continue to cycle through delight, disappointment, and curiosity

- Learning and looking below the surface of things are your responsibility

- If the seminar began with the rocks in "The Jar" [1.03]: You started with rocks, now you've progressed to pebbles

"So you can end with almost any story," said the Apprentice, "provided you have a clear intention in mind, and the story supports what you want your group or audience to do with the information that you've been sharing with them."

Middles and topics
"Exactly! Now how could you use stories within the overall structure of your communication? For example, if you wanted to use metaphor to illustrate the following topics which stories in the book might you use? The topics are building successful relationships, teaching the power of multi-sensory communication, dealing with attitude problems, and encouraging greater awareness of the teaching-learning process."

Building relationships

"So let me take these one at a time," the Apprentice responded. "I'll start with building relationships, the art of rapport. I'd choose the story called 'The Watermelon' [5.05]. And here are my reasons." The Apprentice turned to the flipchart and wrote:

Frame: *Teaching relationship skills*

Purpose: *To introduce the topic: either tell story before the teaching input without explanation or recap the topic after the teaching input.*

Choice: either without any explanation at all, or you can encourage small group discussion to allow the exploration of key learnings about the topic

Reasons:

- Uses the contrast frame to demonstrate a useful model for building effective relationships against a less than useful model

- Demonstrates the skill of pacing, in other words the art of walking step by step with a person or group to recognise and validate their culture and values before beginning to introduce new information into their reality

- Demonstrates the test for rapport: when you lead, others will follow. If they don't follow, you need to do more pacing. All excellent leaders know how to pace

- Demonstrates the essential art of flexibility. If you want to build effective relationships, you need to adapt your behaviours initially to suit the reality of others. Other stories to support this viewpoint: "Perceptual Positions" [1.15], "The Jam Jar" [5.01], "Behavioural Flexibility" [5.08]

"Very good." The Magician was impressed. "I'm curious. Why would you not explain the meaning of your metaphor?"

"Well. It depends. Sometimes, perhaps, I would. But other times I might let the group discuss it, depending on my outcome, as a possible alternative. But, you know, quite often I have heard a Magician tell a story, and obviously it has something to do with the point she is making. But I don't get the connection. I feel frustrated and my mind keeps going back to it, trying to work out a meaning. Sometimes it's taken me six months to work out what a story means. And it's a great feeling when I finally do. I wouldn't want to take that pleasure of discovery, the AHA!, away from anyone unless there was a really good reason."

Multi-sensory communication

"And sometimes there will be. So tell me how you would use story to introduce me to, or persuade me of, the importance of multi-sensory communication."

"There's loads of stories that will bring the topic of the senses to people's attention. Now let me see. One is the 'The Secret of Success' [3.02] where the Wise One invites the young boy to visit his palace and use all his senses to enjoy the fantastic experience. Then, the Wise One suggests that if we use our senses effectively, by keeping them open and alert, we can begin to understand how the world exists to serve us. The world is a brilliant creation with a huge abundance of resources available for us to learn from and work with, if only we will pay attention to it, both on the surface and in noticing the underlying patterns."

"Excellent. Which other stories would you choose?"

"For the key teaching points, and to show how this information can be applied to improve relationships and communication in personal and professional contexts, naturally I'd use the story called 'Talking the Same Language' [3.07].

"But for motivating a group to pay attention from the very beginning to the importance of multi-sensory communication, there's one particular story I would choose. It asks us to experience for ourselves how powerful the senses are in our thinking patterns, in how we make sense of the world, in how we communicate, and how we influence ourselves and others. That story is 'Food for Thought' [2.08].

"Whenever I read it or hear it, I can't stop myself getting hungry enough to eat a horse. I see the food, I smell it, I can feel the textures of it in my mouth, and I can taste all the different flavours. I can even hear my jaw clicking as I chew the cheese. And above all, I'm always amazed that I can start salivating all over the place just by listening to the words of this story."

"Quite right," said the Magician. "The brain can't tell the difference between what is real and what is imagined. Even though there's no food there, your brain responds as if there is. That's a powerful knowledge for an excellent and ethical communicator. You can use words to move people to powerful places and experiences to test out—in their lived experience—the validity of what you are saying."

"Gosh!" said the Apprentice, looking at his watch and thinking now of dinner. "All this thinking and talking of food is exhausting. I don't really feel like talking about attitude right now. Can we do it tomorrow?"

Tomorrow the Magician had other pressing engagements. She rummaged in her bag and fished out a bar of chocolate.

"Perhaps *I* can deal with the topic of attitude, and then afterwards you can tell me how you might critique certain aspects of the teaching-learning loop through the application of story and metaphor. Is that a deal?"

"S'a deal!" said the Apprentice, taking the proffered chocolate bar. He leaned back in his chair, removed the packaging, took a mouth-filling bite, and eagerly awaited the words of the Master.

Attitude

"There are many ways in which people allow negative attitudes to limit their possibilities and potential," said the Magician. "Some of the commonest are lack of commitment, resistance to learning and change, adherence to convention, making assumptions, blaming rather than taking responsibility, using the notion of perfection as an excuse not to take action, expecting something for nothing, and refusing to invest in themselves."

"So which stories might be useful for encouraging such people to reframe their thinking and perceptions?" asked the Apprentice.

"You will find for yourself many such stories in the book. Some will be immediately apparent to you; others you will discover in relation to particular attitude problems that arise as you communicate with individuals and groups."

"Can you give me some examples of stories that are immediately apparent?"

"For perfectionists the story called 'The Perfectionist' [2.13] is pretty transparent. And I always enjoy the story about Werner Bichlmeyer and his initial resistance to learning something he later became an expert at, 'That Won't Work' [5.09]."

"What are some of your favourites?" pressed the Apprentice.

"One of my favourite stories about attitude, and one I use in many different contexts, is a metaphor first developed by the Wizard Roberto Assagioli, a psychiatrist. I found a version of it in a book by another great storyteller, Rachel Remen. It's the story called 'Three Stonemasons' [4.01]."

"So what's so special about this story? What does it teach?"

The Magician turned to the flipchart and wrote:

Key inferences:
- Attitude is the responsibility of each individual

- What you get from life matches what you put into it

- Creativity is innate to all of us; but certain attitudes and a sense of discipline are required to release it

- Each one of us is part of greater and wider systems

- Rewards are not only material

- There are many ways to worship and to celebrate creation

- Patterns and structures underlie the surface of all behaviours

- Each of us can learn what we want or need from a story; they are not prescriptive, merely suggestive

"Of course, there are many other things beside, but for now these will do."

Assumptions and conventions

"You mentioned assumptions, and adherence to convention, earlier. In what way are these attitude problems?" asked the Apprentice.

"Eventually we all have to make assumptions in the process of communicating with others because we can never truly know another person's inner map of reality. What we can do is ensure that we gather sufficient quality information about another's inner map before we take action on the assumptions we are making. In other words we need to gather quality evidence through our senses."

"Ah yes, now I remember the words of the Wizard Bandler, 'Successful communication is 95% information gathering followed by 5% action'."

"A useful guideline. Most people gather only about 20% of the information they need and wonder why they miscommunicate and misunderstand each other so often. A story that deals with this topic is 'Assumptions' [4.12]."

"And I would choose the story about Picasso [5.14] to deal with the issue of convention," added the Young Apprentice.

"Excellent. And for what reasons?" asked the Master.

This time the Apprentice turned to the flipchart and wrote:

Key inferences ["Picasso"]:

- Convention maintains stability in society; this is important *and* limiting

- Convention programmes us to see and experience things in certain ways

- As there are other ways in which things can be seen and understood it is necessary that conventions are not regarded as the truth but merely as holding forms

- Many conventions taken literally are quite ridiculous

- What conventions run your life?

- Art can teach us much, yet art is not the truth and has its own conventions

- Question the validity of everything

"Very interesting," said the Magician. "I see you have been paying attention to your lessons in Philosophy 101." The Apprentice blushed. He wasn't sure if this was a compliment.

"Well, that's what I think, anyway." The Apprentice defended himself.

Responsibility

"I think your ideas are excellent. And I'm very pleased that you're prepared to take responsibility for your views. Teachers, parents, managers, leaders in one form or another often ask me how to deal with the blame culture that seems to be so pervasive in so many of our organisations and cultures. A story is an excellent tool since it questions the unwanted behaviour indirectly. Yet the message is inescapable. It is important, to effect real and lasting change, that we give space to the 'blamer', the one who is refusing to take or accept responsibility, to think through their behaviours and actions for themselves. Lasting change and real understanding come only from within."

"So which stories might you use to encourage responsibility?"

"You'll find several in the book. Some are more indirect such as 'Heaven and Hell' [4.10]. The most obvious is 'The Flood' [4.07]. I particularly like this one because it makes so apparent the abundance of resources that exist around us and that enable us to achieve the results that we want. It suggests that if we don't take advantage of these external resources, by using our intelligence and awareness, it is nobody's fault but our own."

"But sometimes," protested the Apprentice, "things happen to us, through no fault of our own, which are completely out of our control. Why should we take responsibility for that?"

"True," said the Magician, "but as I have said so many times before, who is it that will have to take responsibility for dealing with the situation?"

The Apprentice wisely took responsibility for taking the Master's point.

Personal investment, value, and money
"Let me give you another example which combines responsibility with the question of value, worth, personal investment, and money. Last week I ran three seminars, one after the other, on different communication strategies, which were open to the public.

"One woman arrived just in time for the last seminar although she had paid for all three. She had made the decision that it was more important to attend to certain other things in her busy professional life than attend the first two programmes. She expressed the idea that it would have been better if the seminars had been run later in the day (so that she could have attended), and she was also concerned that she had wasted her money by missing the first two."

"So what did you do?"

"Quite by chance the topic of this last seminar was The Magic of Metaphor. My main concern was to put her at ease so that she could settle down. I wanted her to learn from the workshop rather than continue worrying about life treating her unfairly. I had told the story of 'The Flood' early in the programme although in reference to another context brought up by another member of the group. Nevertheless, it was clear, through paying attention to her non-verbal signals, that she was making connections with her situation. Here, I chose a particular story, 'The Flood', to deal with two completely different contexts at the same time.

"Later, I addressed her situation concerning value for money directly. It was true she had paid three times as much for the course as anybody else. But if what she learned on the course made a significant difference in her life, enabled her to communicate more effectively, and win more contracts to increase her professional prestige and personal wealth, what would be the true worth of the course? Having framed the situation in this way, I then shared the story of 'Knowing Where to Tap' [3.03]."

"What did she do then?"

"She invited me for an excellent lunch and then grilled me about all the things she had missed in the earlier seminars. A fair exchange."

Adapting the stories

"Do you use the stories as they are? Or do you sometimes adapt and change them?"

"The stories are presented as written English. Written English and spoken English are two different languages, so I suggest you always tell the stories in your own words. However, if you want to read them the first few times to gain confidence, or to make sure you use certain words or language structures for particular reasons, then reading them is also acceptable."

"And what about changing elements of the content?" pursued the Apprentice.

"That is a choice you make, depending on circumstances, relationship, environment, context, and other variable factors. It is perfectly acceptable, sometimes even necessary, to change the content of the stories."

"Can you give some examples?"

"Let's take the previous story, 'Knowing Where to Tap' [3.03]. In this story a mill owner's steam boiler has broken down and nobody can fix it. When I told the story in the context we talked about earlier I changed the boiler to a tractor and set the story in a farming context. This was because the city where the seminar took place was in the centre of a huge farming region. Instead of production being halted, the crops could not be harvested and were in danger of rotting in the field.

"When the farmer complained about the cost of the repairs, the mechanic drew attention to the fact that the value of the harvest was more than a thousand times the fee demanded. A change in a system may be small, but if it releases the potential of the system what value can you put on it? Knowing where to tap is an art gained through years of experience, discipline, and personal investment. For extra immediacy I also changed the pounds sterling in the original to the local currency."

"So your changes can be quite brutal?"

"The central question to ask yourself is, what is my outcome, my purpose, my intention? Once you are clear about these, use whatever methods and strategies are appropriate to achieve them.

"There are several stories that spring to mind that I frequently change according to context. In a business context I might adapt the story 'The Jar' [1.03] to focus on time management issues.

"In the story 'The Grammarian' [4.05], in which different kinds of thinking are compared, I might change the roles of Schoolmaster and Businessman to Owl and Rabbit to make it more generic. Or I could adapt the story to be about the relative skills, behaviours, and thinking patterns of a farmer and a lawyer marooned on a desert island.

"In the story entitled 'Lunchtime Learning' [1.14] I could change the last lines of the story in a variety of different ways. In the original the Mother Mouse says, 'Never underestimate the importance of learning a second language.'

"Here are some alternative endings appropriate to different contexts:

'Never underestimate the importance of *knowing your enemy.*'
'Never underestimate the importance of *making your presentation powerfully.*'
'Never underestimate the importance of *having more than one choice in life.*'
"Never underestimate the importance of *shifting your perceptual position.*'

"And so on."

The Apprentice waited expectantly for more. The Magician held the silence and finally reminded her Apprentice of the deal they had struck earlier.

"And you are going to share some of your favourite stories on the topic of a subject close to your heart, learning. Perhaps in relation to some of your experiences at the hands of several of your teachers both before and during your time at the Wizards Academy."

Learning and teaching

The Apprentice brushed a few chocolate crumbs from his lips and thought for a moment or two. He then connected to a higher power and began.

"You've already touched on so many areas that I have come to understand are really important to successful learning and the qualities of an excellent teacher and communicator. These areas are to do with having a positive set of attitudes and beliefs, such as those described in 'Three Stonemasons' [4.01], 'You Have It or You Don't' [4.02], and 'Einstein and Intelligence' [1.07]. Equally it is useful to avoid negative or limiting attitudes and beliefs such as those set out in 'The Chicken and the Eagle' [4.14] and 'Two Little Boys' [3.06].

"You have mentioned communicators, which includes some teachers, whose thinking is partial, limited, and insufficiently flexible to meet the challenges posed by the real world as in the story of 'The Grammarian' [4.05]. Some teachers and communicators talk too much, not giving enough space for their students to contribute, as described in the story of 'The Priest' [2.03]. Some teachers and communicators falsely think there is only one right answer, only one way to think and behave, as in the story of 'Thinking Differently' [3.05].

"I have learned that learning is a discipline and that it can take time, application, and a sense of purpose. These lessons can be found in stories like 'Three Steps to Success' [1.08], 'Gary Player' [3.14], and 'Cutting Remarks' [5.03].

"Learning becomes easy and accelerated when you learn from observing and listening to experts, modelling their behaviours, and responding to feedback. These messages are to be found in 'Three Steps to Success' [1.08], 'The Warrior of the Shadows' [1.13], and 'Thomas Edison: A strategy for genius' [3.13].

"Learning requires intention, flexibility, and sensory acuity so that you can respond effectively to the process of getting from where you are to where you want to be, as in 'Learning the Rules' [2.12] and 'The Jam Jar' [5.01].

"Each person is unique and learns in their own way. Communicators need to be flexible in order to reach the different styles of people who process information in different ways, and to be respectful of them, their needs, and their contributions. These lessons are to be found in 'The Jar' [1.03], 'Tutta la Vita e Fuori' [2.09], 'Talking the Same Language' [3.07], and 'Walking to Learn' [5.06].

"Finally, learning is a lifelong process. And for me, the real secret to successful and lazy learning, and the ability to discover real fun in the process, is one amazing revelation. That below the surface of everyday experience, and all the multitude of facts that seem so complex and unrelated on the surface, are patterns and structures. I see myself as a detective. Once I discover what these structures and patterns are then the possibilities of learning, understanding, and passing on my knowledge to others becomes not only possible but pleasurable. It is nothing less than a celebration of our capabilities, creativity, and intelligence.

"These are the lessons of 'Real Knowledge' [2.02], 'Designer Genes' [3.01], 'Pebbles' [5.04], and 'Acorns' [5.15]."

"Excellent," said the Master. "You are almost a magician, and I have learned from you. So here is your final task. Show me, what have *you* learned?"

The Apprentice turned to the flipchart, wrote the title *Some Ways to Build Communication and Relationships through Metaphor*, and brainstormed the map on the following page.

The Master took the Apprentice's hand and smiled at him. "Now you know how to begin and continue your journey. Now you know the steps to take towards achieving the excellence you desire. And I know—with purpose, discipline, and the acceptance of feedback—you will achieve it. Are you still hungry?"

Not knowing exactly whether the Master was talking about food or learning, but thinking both, the Apprentice licked his lips and replied, "I'm always hungry."

"Yes," said the Magician, "and that's precisely the magic of metaphor."

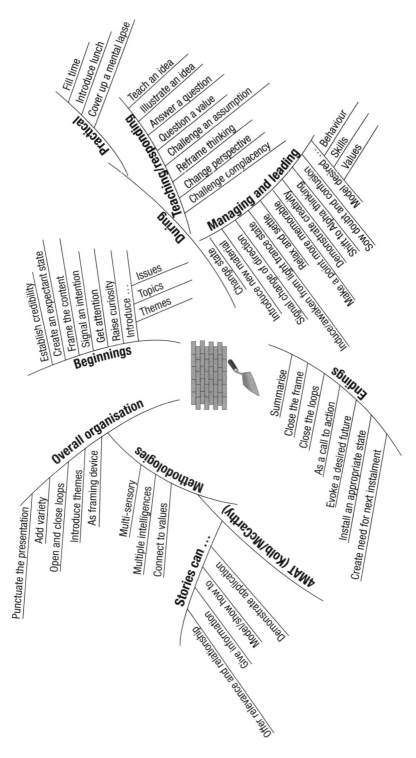

Some Ways to Build Communication and Relationships through Metaphor

Practical
- Fill time
- Introduce lunch
- Cover up a mental lapse

Teaching/responding
- Teach an idea
- Illustrate an idea
- Answer a question
- Question a value
- Challenge an assumption
- Reframe thinking
- Change perspective
- Challenge complacency

During

Managing and leading
- Induce/awaken from light trance state
- Signal change of direction
- Change state
- Relax and settle
- Demonstrate creativity
- Make a point, more memorable
- Shift to Alpha thinking
- Sow doubt and confusion
- Model desired ...
  - Behaviour
  - Skills
  - Values

Beginnings
- Establish credibility
- Create an expectant state
- Frame the content
- Signal an intention
- Get attention
- Raise curiosity
- Introduce ...
  - Issues
  - Topics
  - Themes

Endings
- Summarise
- Close the frame
- Close the loops
- As a call to action
- Evoke a desired future
- Install an appropriate state
- Create need for next instalment

Overall organisation
- Punctuate the presentation
- Add variety
- Open and close loops
- Introduce themes
- As framing device

Methodologies
- Multi-sensory
- Multiple intelligences
- Connect to values
- 4MAT (Kolb/McCarthy)

Stories can ...
- Give information
- Model/show how to
- Demonstrate application
- Offer relevance and relationship

Bibliography

Collections of Stories

Canfield J, Hansen MV. *Chicken Soup for the Soul*. London: Vermillion, 2000.

Morgan J, Rinvolucri M. *Once Upon a Time*. Cambridge: Cambridge University Press, 1983.

Okot p'Bitek. *Hare and Hornbill*. Oxford: Heinemann AWS, 1978.

Peseschkian N. *Oriental Stories as Tools for Psychotherapy*. London: Sterling Press, 1982.

Pinkola Estes C. *Women Who Run with the Wolves*. London: Rider, 1993.

Shah I. *The Way of the Sufi*. London: Penguin Arkana, 1968.

Shah I. *Thinkers of the East*. London: Octagon Press, 1971.

Shah I. *World Tales*. London: Octagon Press, 1991.

Source Books for Stories

Coelho P. *The Alchemist*. London: Thorsons, 1998.

Coelho P. *The Pilgrimage*. London: Thorsons, 1997.

Knight S. *NLP at Work*. London: Nicholas Brealey Publishers, 1995.

Knight S. *NLP Solutions*. London: Nicholas Brealey Publishers, 1999.

Lupton H. *Tales of Wisdom and Wonder*. London: Barefoot Books, 1998.

Lupton H. *The Songs of Birds*. London: Barefoot Books, 2000.

Revell J, Norman S. *In Your Hands*. London: Saffire Press, 1997.

Revell J, Norman S. *Handing Over*. London: Saffire Press, 1999.

Remen R. *Kitchen Table Wisdom*. London: Pan, 1996.

Wright A. *Storytelling with Children*. Oxford: Oxford University Press, 1995.

Books on Various Applications of Metaphor

Berman M, Brown D. *The Power of Metaphor*. Carmarthen: Crown House Publishing, 2000.

Gordon D. *Therapeutic Metaphors*. Capitola, California: Meta Publishing, 1978.

Lakoff G, Johnson M. *Metaphors We Live By*. Chicago: University of Chicago Press, 1980.

Lawley J, Tompkins P. *Metaphors in Mind*. London: Developing Company Press, 2000.

Stimulating Background Reading

Bandler R. *Patterns of the Hypnotic Techniques of Milton H. Erickson*. Portland, Oregon: Metamorphous Press, 1996. MD, Volumes 1, 2.

Bateson G, Bateson MC. *Steps to an Ecology of the Mind*. Chicago: University of Chicago Press, 1972.

Chopra D. *The Way of the Wizard*. London: Rider, 2000.

Erickson M, Rosen S. *My Voice Will Go with You*. London: W W Norton, 1991.

Grinder M. *Righting the Educational Conveyor Belt*. Portland, Oregon: Metamorphous Press, 1991.

Jensen E. *The Learning Brain*. San Diego: The Brain Store Inc., 1994.

Laborde G. *Influencing with Integrity*. Carmarthen: Crown House Publishing, 1998.

Miller G. The Magical Number 7. Plus or Minus 2. *Psychological Review* 1956; 63.

O'Connor J, Seymour J. *Introducing Neuro Linguistic Programming*. London: Aquarian, 1990.

Pirsig, Robert M. *Lila: An Inquiry into Morals*. London: Corgi, 1992.

Pirsig, Robert M. *Zen and the Art of Motorcycle Maintenance: An Inquiry into Values*. London: Vintage, 1989.

Robbins A. *Unlimited Power*. New York: Simon & Schuster, 1986.

Shlain L. *The Alphabet versus the Goddess*. London: Penguin, 2000.

Articles on the Uses and Applications of Stories

Owen N. Presenting Excellence. *English Teaching Professional (ETp)*, Vols 17, 18, 19, 20, October 2000 through July 2001.

Owen, N. Teaching Excellence. *ETp* 1999; Vol. 13, October.

Owen N. *Telling Stories for a Change. New Standpoints*. Paris: Speakeasy Publications, 2000.

Wright A. The Craft of Storytelling. *ETp* 1999; Vol. 13, October.

About Nick Owen

Nick Owen has, at various stages of his life, developed successful and interconnected careers in education, the arts, journalism, overseas development and the world of corporate business. He has lived and worked in Africa, Asia, Latin America, and Europe.

He studied at Durham, Manchester and Oxford universities, is an NLP trainer and Master Practitioner, and holds qualifications in Spiral Dynamics, the Harthill [UK] Leadership Development Framework, and Reversal Theory.

His clients range from FTSE 100 companies to small educational projects in remote regions of the planet.

His main areas of expertise are:

- enhancing professional performance
- enhancing life skills
- understanding how 'messages' are given, received, acted upon or misunderstood
- resolving communication and relationship issues in order to create smoothly functioning organisations
- strengthening individuals and organisations through *horizontal* development; transforming individuals and organisations through *vertical* development
- co-creating models of excellent and appropriate leadership to build organisations in which everyone wants to belong and to which all can contribute.

Nick is Director of Nick Owen Associates offering rigorous development opportunities in the following areas:

Business: communication, presentation, relationships, influence, creativity, cultural awareness, leadership, trainer development, unconditional responsibility, motivation, coaching and mentoring skills

Education:	integral education, appropriate methodologies, leadership, classroom management, creativity, teacher development, motivation, coaching and mentoring skills
Professional development:	tailor-made courses for professionals
Personal development:	tailor-made programmes for individuals including personal life coaching
Executive coaching:	for senior managers
Certification courses:	NLP-based courses, including professionally geared NLP Diploma and Practitioner Programmes

For more information, e-mail Nick Owen at **nick@nickowen.net** or go to **www.nickowen.net**

More Magic of Metaphor

Stories for Leaders, Influencers, Motivators and Spiral Dynamics Wizards

Nick Owen

"… a magical source book for leaders, therapists,
trainers and the curious."

Martin Woods, Head of Leadership Development, Norwich Union Insurance

Our greatest teachers, artists and leaders all use story and
metaphor to put across their 'message' in powerful and
highly memorable ways. This follow up to Nick Owen's best-
selling *The Magic of Metaphor* explores the power of stories to
inspire, inform and transform people's lives. With a particular
emphasis on leadership, the stories in this collection offer
inspiration, inner knowledge and wisdom.

Presented as a metaphorical journey of discovery, *More Magic of
Metaphor* explores the nature of leadership in everyday life and
provides effective tools for influencing, motivating and leading
others with elegance and integrity.

Paperback, 368 pages, ISBN: 978-190442441-3

www.crownhouse.co.uk

The Salmon of Knowledge

Stories for Work, Life, the Dark Shadow, and OneSelf

Nick Owen

A collection of stories, analogies and metaphors that invite us to pause and consider what is really important in our lives, our work, and ourselves. They challenge us to re-connect the different parts of our lives, recognise how easy it is to get distracted by contemporary culture and the pace of modern life, and to pay attention to whatever deeper parts of ourselves seek expression.

The stories invite us to slow down, take more time to reflect, experience the world from wider perspectives, and make wiser and more sustainable choices. They invite us to put ourselves squarely in the centre of the on-going story that is our life, to take greater responsibility for connecting to what serves us, others, and the wider context, and to find a greater variety of ways to express ourselves fully through our life, our work, and everything we can be.

Paperback, 256 pages, ISBN: 978-184590127-1

www.crownhouse.co.uk